Alfred's Teach Yourself to Play Drums 2nd Edition

PATRICK WILSON

PREFACE

Learning any musical instrument is not simple. It takes time to develop skills through practice and patience.

Without question, the *best* way to learn how to play an instrument is with the help of a good private instructor—someone who is not only an experienced player, but also capable of recognizing problems in a student's playing and then correcting them with the least amount of grief and hassle. (Realistically, very few of today's finest and most versatile players reached their level of achievement without the help of one or more teachers.)

For any number of reasons you may not be able to take private lessons now. Hopefully you'll reach a point where playing is such an important priority in your life that lessons will be a "must." One way or another, you'll find ways around those obstacles preventing private instruction.

The purpose of *Teach Yourself to Play Drums* is to give you the best help available until private instruction becomes practical. Keep in mind it is not a *replacement* for private drumset instruction, but an alternative for the time being. In this book there is enough diverse material—some easy, some very challenging—for *years* of study.

—Patrick Wilson

NOTE TO TEACHERS

While this book is designed for personal instruction, it may also be very successful in your studio. If you've been looking for a thorough, step-by-step method for teaching all the basics, covering a broad array of music styles, look no further. *Teach Yourself to Play Drums* makes teaching easier!

About the CD

A companion audio recording is available including many of the drum patterns and fills (which may have been packaged with the book you purchased). It features play-along pieces, offering you the experience of actually playing with a band. The right channel of the recording can be turned off, which has the drum track, allowing you to become the drummer for the "Play Now!" and "Sitting In" sections! This disc will greatly facilitate teaching yourself to play drums.

Throughout the book a CD logo (shown above) indicates there are companion recorded examples.

Alfred Music
P.O. Box 10003
Van Nuys, CA 91410-0003
alfred.com

ISBN-10: 0-7390-9902-7 (Book & CD)
ISBN-13: 978-0-7390-9902-5 (Book & CD)

Overhead drumset photo by Larry Lytle

CONTENTS

BIOGRAPHY

Patrick Wilson possesses that rare combination of diverse talent and determination to succeed at any music endeavor. He has won conducting and concerto competitions, scored music for film and TV, composed for concert halls and theaters, and has penned numerous music articles. As a drummer and percussionist, he has worked with an entire spectrum of artists and has played diverse venues such as the Hollywood Bowl and Chicago's Orchestra Hall. For this book, he draws upon years of teaching experience in the Midwest.

This book is dedicated to my parents; I am a musician because of their musical talents.

ACKNOWLEDGMENTS

For their support, I wish to thank Morty and Iris Manus, John O'Reilly and the entire Alfred staff, especially Sharon Aaronson and Gayle Kowalchyk. Joel Leach and Dave Black spent hours dissecting the manuscript, making the book much stronger; their efforts were very much appreciated, and I am indebted to them.

The editorial contributions of Susan Christiansen and Elizabeth Churchville were invaluable, as was the help of Kevin Mitchell. Questioning every move, David Smooke kept production on track and made several editorial improvements. Sue Hartman and especially Bruce Goldes added their considerable talents in producing the interior, while Ted Engelbart put together a marvelous cover. Jeff Leland shot superb interior pictures with the aid of Ruth McKinney. Mary Ann Graham and Sean Stackpool were very patient models for the interior photos, and I thank Greg McKinney for his efforts with the interior diagrams.

Respect must be paid to the parade of talented drummers and percussionists that I have admired over the years, among them, teachers and friends Al O'Connor, Richard Cheadle, Steve Houghton, Dale Anderson, Ken Watson, Jay Wanamaker, Ed Poremba, Bill Wilson, Bill Drake, Gary Donnelly (a personally inspirational drummer), Bill Gade, Jeff Kestenbaum, John McCullough and Bert Ferntheil ("The Legend").

And, finally, I am most grateful to best friends Bruce Frausto and Bob Wake.

CD MUSICIANS

Featuring freelance drummer Dave Tull (played with Maynard Ferguson, Jack Sheldon, Buddy Greco among others)

Keyboards: Greg Hilfman
Guitar: Steve Hall
Bass: Tre Henry
Saxophones/Clarinet:
    Gordon Brisker
Trumpet/Flugelhorn:
    Larry Gillespie
Trombone: Rob Wren
Fiddle: Dennis Fetchet
Pedal Steel Guitar:
    Jim Eaton

PART I Getting Started

A BRIEF HISTORY OF THE DRUMS

Excluding the human voice, it is generally accepted that the drum is the oldest musical instrument. It has existed almost as long as humanity. The primitive beginning of the drum was simply a portion of a hollowed log struck with sticks. Later, additional resonance was attained by stretching an animal skin across one end, tautly fastened with vine "twine" and wood pegs. At this time, drums were used more in a practical fashion than today—for coded, rhythmic communication across distances, and, later, for tribal ceremonies.

The modern drumset is an outgrowth of the Afro-American funeral bands of the South. These small "walking" bands (which still exist in New Orleans) traditionally accompanied a funeral to the ceremony and consisted of a few horns, a snare drummer and a bass drummer. After the ceremony, it was common for the band to regroup for a follow-up celebration. A rather creative drummer (whose name has long been forgotten) figured he could play both the snare and bass drums if he only had a stand and foot pedal.

Having achieved this, it was a short step to add various cymbals, some tom-toms and a few other sound effect instruments (such as a woodblock, cowbell and temple blocks mounted on the bass drum) to play music of the early 20th century. This music included ragtime, fox-trots, and Dixieland, as well as music for vaudeville theater pits, movie houses and, later, radio. A standard set of simple traps was developed: a snare, a cymbal or

▲ *A logo (log drum) being played in Western Samoa.*

◄ *African peg drum and beater.*

▼ *Early brass band of Lutcher, Louisiana.*

two, a hi-hat (two cymbals, one atop the other, mounted on a pedal mechanism, which opens and closes them), one or two tom-toms and a bass drum with a pedal beater. During the Swing Era of the late '30s and the '40s, the big-band drummers shed the sound effects.

It wasn't until the early years of rock in the '60s that the drumset was significantly modified. Rock drummers added more cymbals, toms and even another bass drum at times. Later, electronics found its way into the drumset or "kit" (as it is sometimes called). In the 1980s, a set was created consisting solely of rubber pads (and hardware), which triggered an electronic device when struck (see page 8). Even cymbals could now be produced electronically. This device—a synthesizer of sorts—could be programmed to reproduce the more familiar drum sounds, plus many new and unusual ones as well. This innovation allowed a drummer to play many different-sounding drumsets with just a single set of pads. The further electronic development of sampling—the ability to digitally record and store any type of acoustic sound, which could later be recalled—made the drummer's library of sounds limited only by his or her imagination.

Today's drummer may use acoustic kits, electronic sets or a combination of the two. Whatever the preference, the basic principles for playing remain the same. This book will explain those principles to help achieve your goal—teaching yourself to play drums!

▲ *One of the fathers of percussion, the late Roy Knapp, in his Chicago-based studio. Configuration from the early days of radio.*

▲ *Neil Peart's setup includes electronics.*

GETTING STARTED — WHAT TO PLAY (SELECTING YOUR INSTRUMENTS)

ACOUSTIC DRUMS

A drumset consists of four elements: drums, cymbals, hardware (stands, mounting devices and pedals) and a stool or "throne." For your first set, you will need at least the following:

Drums

Snare—a relatively small drum, characterized by snares (almost always wire) stretched across the bottom head. A lever on the side of the drum releases or engage the snares. (Releasing them creates, in effect, a somewhat high-pitched tom.)

Tom-tom (or "tom")—a mid-sized drum, pitched somewhere between the snare and bass. It is highly preferable, though not essential, to have at least two toms: one mounted on the bass drum and the other, larger one a "floor tom," which usually has self-contained hardware. (Another practical arrangement for positioning tom-toms includes racks.)

Bass—the largest drum, which sits on the floor and is played with a pedal.

Cymbals

Ride—a large, relatively thick cymbal (19 to 22 inches in diameter).

Crash—a mid-sized cymbal (16 to 18 inches in diameter) with a quick response and often a rather quick decay when struck hard. If your budget does not allow for this cymbal, you may get by without it, but it will be sorely missed and should be added at the first opportunity.

Hi-Hat—a set of two rather small cymbals (13 to 15 inches in diameter) which can vary in weight/thickness, depending on the desired

▲ *Acoustic Set (front).*

sound. Sometimes the bottom cymbal is slightly thicker than the top.

Hardware

Snare Stand—obviously, to support the snare drum.

Cymbal Stands—one for the ride, the other for the crash. (On some older sets, hardware for a ride-cymbal stand is attached to the bass drum.) Wing nuts, with felt washers placed above and below the cymbal, keep them from flying off the stand. Small plastic sleeves, which fit around the threads at the top of the stand, keep bare metal from touching bare metal, preventing the cymbal from cracking (see page 87 on care and maintenance). Telescopic stands, or "boom" stands, are often used for larger, heavier cymbals and

allow greater flexibility when positioning them.

Hi-Hat Stand—a particular cymbal stand with a tension spring in its shaft (which is usually adjustable) and a foot pedal to lower the top cymbal onto the bottom one. A "clutch" and felt pads hold the top cymbal on a rod which moves with the pedal; the lower cymbal rests on another felt pad and holder. The stand includes an adjustment on the bottom cymbal holder to offset the angle of the lower cymbal. This prevents the two cymbals from locking together in a vacuum (airlock) when they are brought together with the pedal. The bottom cymbal is available with drilled holes to alleviate airlock.

Labels in image:
- Crash Cymbal
- Ride Cymbal
- Snare
- Hi-Hat Angle Adjustment
- Hi-Hat Tension Adjustment
- Hi-Hat Pedal
- Bass Drum Pedal
- Bass Drum Pedal Tension Adjustment
- Bass Drum Beater
- Stool

▲ *Acoustic Set (back).*

Tom-Tom Mount—holds the tom in place and is generally connected to the bass drum shell. In the case of a floor tom, rods or "legs" elevate it off the floor.

Bass Drum Pedal—connects, via a clamp, to the rim of the bass drum.

Bass Drum Spurs—two rods which keep the drum from tilting side to side or creeping forward.

Miscellaneous

Stool or **Throne**—a small padded seat with height adjustment.

Rug or **Mat**—necessary for protecting the floor, as well as the bass drum bottom. It also keeps the bass drum from creeping forward following each impact of the pedal's beater, so choose something that will not slide on a smooth surface.

Sticks—a possible beginner size is "5A" or "5B," but anything in that range is good. (Note: There is no standard system for classifying assorted stick types.) However, a stick bigger than "2B" is too clumsy. It is wise to resist selecting too small a stick because the muscles in the fingers, hands and wrist will better develop with a little weight. In addition, the slightly heavier stick will bounce higher (beneficial!) and last a little longer. Sticks with plastic nylon tips were created to give a more articulated sound on cymbals, and they also protect the wood tip. Sticks with or without nylon tips are both fine, but realize that each one creates a different type of sound, particularly on cymbals. When purchasing sticks, check for warped wood by rolling them on a flat surface (which most reputable dealers should allow you to do).

Metronome—see page 24.

Cases (optional)—if you will be moving your drums around to gigs and rehearsals, these will greatly cut down on wear and tear, make storage easier, keep hardware organized and assist with transporting equipment.

Rack Stands (optional)—depending on the amount of additional equipment you have, this hardware can be substituted for several single stands as it is capable of holding several toms and sometimes cymbals too.

Drum Key or **Lug Wrench** (a must!)—the purpose of this small tool is to turn the lugs, pulling the drum hoop to tighten the drumhead or loosening it to remove one (see page 88). While it is a bit more expensive, the advantage of a wrench is that it's easier on the hands and easier to use.

Gloves (optional)—some drummers, especially heavy metal players, sport athletic gloves (often the kind weight lifters use to protect their hands and give them a better grip when the hands perspire). Drummers whose hands perspire quite a bit may want to consider trying them out. Realize that gloves can also function as a fashion statement for the player (whether your hands get slippery or not). If you like the idea, use them while you practice in order to get used to playing with them.

WHAT TO PLAY
(continued)

ELECTRONIC DRUMS

You will need the equivalent of the basic acoustic drum sounds (see two previous pages), so a set of three or four pads will be necessary in place of the corresponding acoustic drums. Cords are plugged into output jacks on the pads which connect to a "brain." The brain is the synthesizer that creates the various sounds triggered by playing on the pads. The brain connects to an amplifier, which in turn is connected to headphones or speakers in order to hear the sounds. Cymbals will be the same as an acoustic setup (though if you're really into an electronic sound, the cymbals may be pads too). Hardware will differ only where the pads are concerned, but will function similarly. A rug or mat is still recommended, and choice of sticks is the same for both electronic and acoustic drums, although plastic-tipped sticks will have no effect if pads are use for cymbal sounds.

▲ *5-Piece Electronic Drum Set (minus hi-hat).*

BUYING EQUIPMENT
New Versus Used

There are two rather obvious ways to acquire the instruments: purchasing new equipment from a dealer or buying it used from a dealer or private individual.

In either case, it is always wise to shop around and to avoid "off brands." Buying name brands will help greatly should any hardware need maintenance or replacing.

The advantage in working with a reputable dealer is the service. Such a dealer can assist you with questions you may later have, such as setting up equipment, and can replace faulty merchandise since a warranty is usually provided. If you purchase from a private party, it may be advisable to have setting up and tearing down the set demonstrated, as well as checking the equipment thoroughly. (Imagine the disappointment after handing over the money and driving home to try out your set only to discover you can't put it together!) When shopping used, check to see that all hardware operates and is in good condition (no bent screws, rust, stripped threads, etc.).

HOW-TO-PLAY
BASICS

SETTING UP

On pages 6 and 7, you saw how drumset components are positioned relative to one another. Some drum and cymbal manufacturers have literature available, which shows various artists' setups. It is your decision as to how you place the instruments, depending not only on the instruments you have, but also on *personal preference and comfort*. This is the key. What may be good for a drummer you idolize may not be right for you.

All the instruments should be easily reachable. Your kit should be centralized to minimize reaching, stretching and twisting. Hardware enables you to tilt or angle the instruments to *your* liking. Take advantage of this! As you begin to play and gradually improve, chances are that you will find better ways to position the instruments.

GET A GRIP!

There are two grips commonly used: traditional and matched.

One is not "better" than the other. The traditional grip is more common among jazz drummers and those players who come from a more "traditional" background.* On the other hand (no pun intended!), the matched grip evolved from rock players in the '60s.

It has been argued that the traditional grip allows more finesse while the matched grip offers more power. You may wish to experiment, but understand there are drummers who use both grips, depending on their needs at the moment. Some switch grips while playing! The choice is yours…there is no right or wrong decision.

▲ *Traditional grip.*

▲ *Matched grip.*

* This often implies a study of *rudiments*. (Rudiments are specific, standardized exercises which build technique, endurance and strength, while giving the drummer "licks" which can be applied to playing.) For further study, *International Drum Rudiments* by Rob Carson and Jay Wanamaker contains all drum rudiments. (See listing on page 92.)

HOW-TO-PLAY BASICS
(continued)

THE RIGHT HAND

Traditional & Matched Grip

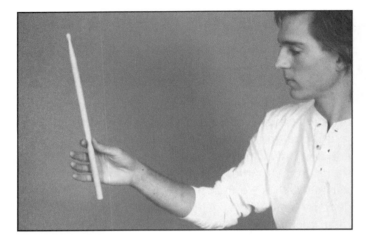

Whether you choose traditional or matched grip, the right hand is the same.

Hold the stick between your thumb and index finger about 5 inches from the back end of the stick. The stick should be parallel to your palm. The index finger should naturally curve around the stick.

Allow the remaining fingers to curve in a relaxed manner around the stick (as with the index finger). They should not completely close around the stick, but should gently rest against it. Nothing should feel forced, but should seem relaxed and fairly natural.

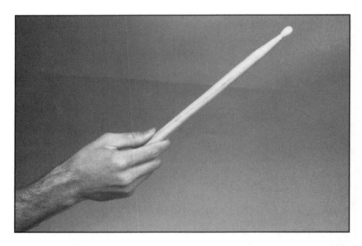

With your palm facing parallel to the floor, the right hand should look like this.

With your palm facing up, the grip should look like this.

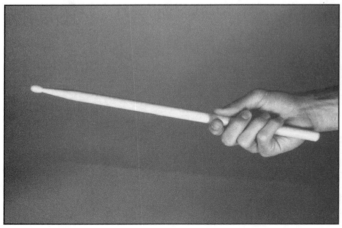

THE LEFT HAND—

Traditional Grip

With the hand perpendicular to the floor, hold the stick with the thumb in the "pocket" (between your thumb and first finger) about two inches from the butt end of the stick.

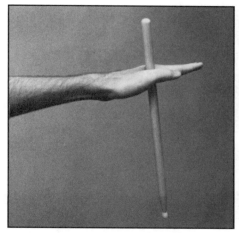 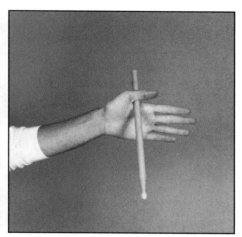

Close your ring finger and little finger, then turn the palm up, allowing the stick to lie on the ring finger. The thumb should curve a bit.

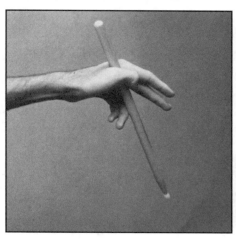 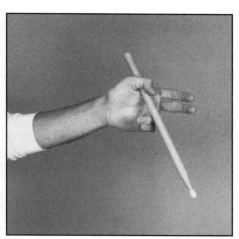

Allow the middle finger and index finger to curve over the stick naturally. Keep the hand relaxed!

 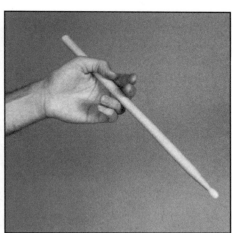

THE LEFT HAND—

Matched Grip

The left hand will "match" (as the name of the grip implies) the right.

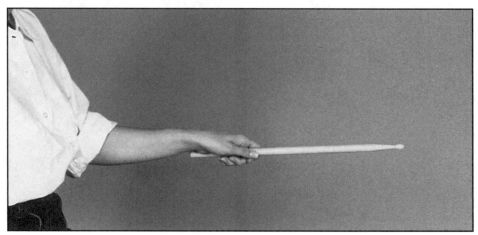

USING YOUR GRIP—THE WRIST

When playing, the action is made primarily with the wrist. (The fingers play a significant role, but that comes a bit later.)

Very little arm motion is needed. Even when playing loud, little arm motion is necessary.

Certain styles of drumming—heavy metal, for instance—promote movement for visual effect. If that's what you're into, great!—but realize it isn't required.

The most important concept here is to STAY RELAXED! Try to be very conscious of when your arms, wrists and fingers become tense… then, back off! It is possible to damage tendons if you do not learn to stay relaxed while playing.

THE RIGHT-HAND WRIST MOTION

Matched & Traditional

1. Without tapping on any surface, bend at the wrist so the stick moves upward.

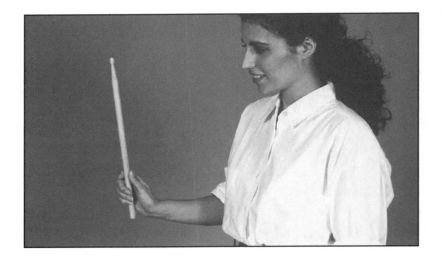

2. Relax the wrist, allowing the stick to drop parallel to the floor.

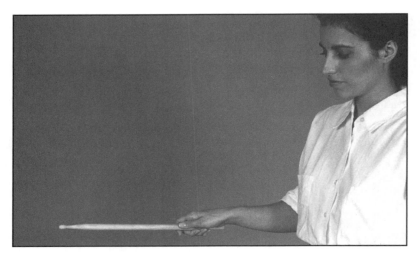

Now repeat #1 and #2 a few times. The stick should move straight up and down. It shouldn't "slice" at an angle.

▲ *The right way—Straight up and down movement.*

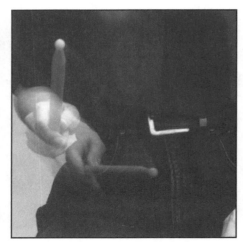

▲ *The wrong way—slicing at an angle.*

THE LEFT-HAND WRIST MOTION

Matched

Identical to the motion used in the right hand (see previous page).

Traditional

1. Without tapping on any surface, rotate the wrist less than a quarter turn bringing the stick tip up a few inches.

2. Rotate the wrist back to its original position bringing the stick downward.

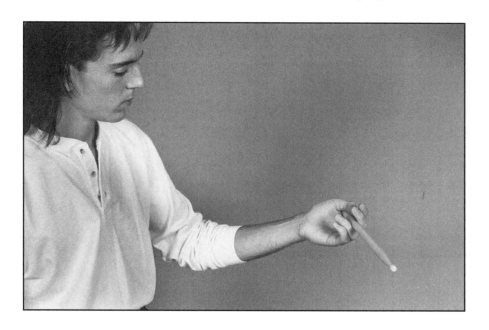

Now repeat #1 and #2 a few times. As with the right hand, the stick should move straight up and down and should not be moving at an angle (see bottom of previous page). Because the grip with this hand is less natural than with the right, it may take some practice achieving a straight up and down stick motion with comfort, while keeping the wrist, hand and fingers relaxed.

Now, let's try it on a drum!

USING YOUR GRIP — THE FINGERS

Seated at your drumset, repeat the exercises on the previous two pages for your particular grip as follows. This time, however, hit your snare rather than just move the sticks in the air.

R = right hand

1.

L = left hand

2.

(alternating hands)

3.

You will notice that there is a natural tendency for the stick to bounce back when you hit the drum. It is no different from the way a ball bounces. If you drop a basketball, gravity pulls it down, then it rebounds back up. You don't have to pull the ball up; it naturally occurs.

This is how drums are played. You need force (a bit of muscle along with gravity) to get the stick moving down—almost none when playing soft!—then simply "catch it" on the rebound. This is where the fingers come into play. They act to catch the stick on the rebound about 2 inches above the drumhead.

Let's look at each hand…

THE RIGHT-HAND FINGERS

With the upstroke, the fingers should release the stick.

They remain this way until the moment after the stick hits the surface. Then, the fingers quickly close to catch the stick as it completes the rebound.

 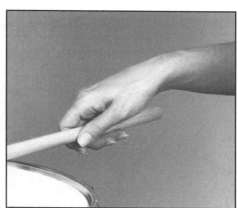

THE LEFT-HAND FINGERS

Matched

Identical to the motion used in the right hand.

Traditional

In similar fashion to the concept with the right hand, the index and middle fingers release the stick with the upstroke. The stick no longer rests on the ring finger. It is "airborne," held only by the thumb.

Just after the stick hits the surface, the wrist turns back to its

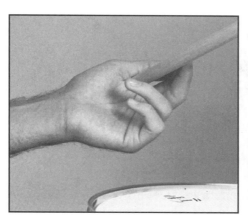 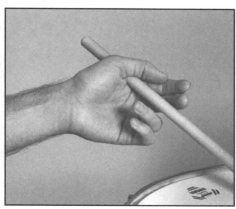

original position (about 2 inches above the drumhead) and the ring finger resumes contact while the index and middle fingers curl back to catch the stick.

This action must become natural with each hand so it occurs without having to think about it. The only way to achieve this is through practice (see page 17).

Technique ...Builder... **1** **INTRODUCTION TO THE SINGLE-STROKE ROLL**

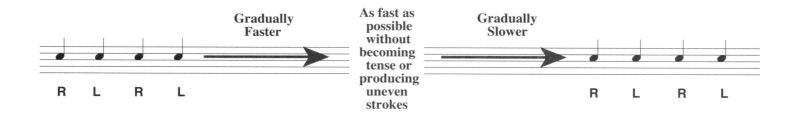

Gradually Faster

As fast as possible without becoming tense or producing uneven strokes

Gradually Slower

R L R L   R L R L

PRACTICE TIP While it may seem elementary, this is a very important exercise because you are laying the foundation for your technique. Keep the strokes even. Remember, *always stay relaxed!*

Bad habits are hard to break, so be patient when you practice. Doing so will mean you won't have to correct bad habits and relearn the right way later.

CD Tracks 1–32

PLAY NOW!

If you have purchased the recording, you will be able to quickly learn a few basic beats, including rock, country and jazz. Simply listen to the recording, following the step-by-step instructions.

— Basic Rock Beat: Tracks 2–12

— Basic Country Beat: Tracks 13–21

— Basic Jazz Beat: Tracks 22–32

Should you have any difficulty, or replay the CD and try it again. You'll be surprised at how quickly you'll be playing along with the audio tracks and having fun making music.

As you continue going through this book, you may want to come back to this portion of the recording when the lessons get a little rough. It will provide encouragement when you become discouraged.

YOUR FIRST EXPERIMENTS

DOS AND DON'TS

— **DO** feel free to experiment!

— **DON'T** be afraid to play around with your set, trying to imitate what you may have heard on the radio and recordings, what you've seen on music videos, in concerts or elsewhere.

— **DO** try and figure out beats and patterns you may have in your head, if possible.

— **DON'T** get frustrated when you can't figure something out. As you go through this book, many things will gradually become apparent.

— **DO** practice slowly and gradually build up speed and **DO** be patient.

— **DO** try to stay relaxed!

— **DON'T** overdo it and strain your muscles.

— **DO** adjust the position of your drums and stands when you have to stretch unnaturally.

— **DON'T** keep your drumset in a certain position just because it "looks neat" or because some other drummer uses a certain setup.

REMOVING BOTTOM HEADS

You've probably seen drummers who play sets with the bottom heads removed on toms as well as the front of bass drums. This creates a sound which is less resonant (generally speaking). It also makes tuning the drums simpler because there is one less head to deal with. If you want less "ringing" to your kit, experiment by removing the bottom head to one of your toms. Once you fiddle with the tuning of one tom with the bottom head removed and decide you like that sound, you may want to take the time to try it with the remaining toms and bass drum.

MUFFLING

Many drums include some device to deaden the ring of a drum. Use of these devices are solely up to you based on the type of sound you prefer. There are a few drummers who also will use tape as a method to dampen sound further. The net effect is an extremely dry sound with almost no ring. One big drawback to this is the sticky residue left on the head should the player change his or her mind.

Almost all drummers will apply some dampening to the bass drum. This may involve pillows inside the drum, removing the front head, using factory-made dampening rings, cloth strips fixed to one or both heads with tape, front drumheads with a hole "built-in," as well as tape.

Again, you should experiment to see what fits your sound.

One further note, should you ever want to record in a studio, dampening will be a prime consideration. Every kit requires careful microphone placement, combined with close attention to muffling techniques.

HOW TO DEAL WITH NOISE

The biggest curse of your newfound love is that everyone else seems to hate the noise! You will probably want to maintain a practice schedule during times when it is least offensive to others-or you'll be *told* to do so by newfound enemies!

Here are a few suggestions that may help you from becoming the least popular person in your living space, if not the neighborhood:

— Muffle your drums with cloth and tape or just tape applied to the heads; cymbals can be deadened with duct or masking tape. (Realize, however, that the glue on the tape may be a bit difficult to clean off later.)

— It is common to remove the front bass drum head and place a pillow inside, either leaving the head off or replacing it.

— Use commercial rubber practice pads to muffle the sound (instead of cloth or tape). These pads can be placed on top of the drums, and are very easy to throw on or off the drums.

— "Soundproof" your practice area by hanging old carpets, blankets or other acoustic material on the walls.

— Use a commercial practice pad set. The added cost for this set will be offset by less wear on your "real" drumset.

LEARNING FROM THE BOOK

THE "P" WORD— *PRACTICING!*

The downfall of any musician is often the lack of discipline necessary to maintain a regular schedule of practicing. Anyone starting out is highly motivated, but this can wear off. The simple and often painful truth is that you must practice to become good. If you are playing purely for pleasure, you will still need to keep a regular schedule to get anywhere.

The trick is to find a time every day for *at least 20 minutes* to work on your drumset. (Less dedicated players can get by practicing only four or five days a week.) Short of illness or an emergency, don't accept any excuses for not practicing. Make a schedule and stick to it! Once you get in the habit, it becomes easier to stay with the commitment.

You should read page 90 now if you've never taken music lessons. This will help you understand how to teach yourself.

FEATURES IN THIS BOOK

 "Mini Music Lessons" are shortcuts to understanding music. They concisely explain key musical concepts and ideas.

 The "Daily Workouts" are exercises and drill assignments to be done for at least one week. When you reach one, you should stop at that place in the book and follow the routine daily for a full week or more. Review past material if you wish, but do not go on until you feel you can do the workout with confidence. At times, you may need more than a week to accomplish this, but don't be discouraged. The extra time you invest will payoff later!

There will be "Practice Tips" relating to "Daily Workouts" throughout the book to lead you into good habits (just like the one you saw on page 15). Following these tips will make an enormous difference in your progression as a drummer.

Technique ...Builder... The "Technique Builders" will help develop muscles, coordination and a tension-free style of playing (as the one on page 15).

USING THE CD

 The play-along recording will help you understand how to read music, keep good time (see page 33), and it will demonstrate beats and fills while making practice fun. Be sure to read the information on page 1 if you haven't done so.

It is divided into the following sections:

— "Play Now!" (see previous page).

— Demonstration of exercises and beats.

— "Sitting In" (play-along tracks).

Important: Before each line of music you will hear one or two "count-off" bars. This will set the tempo (see page 24) before you begin playing. You will hear clicks equal in number to one measure of quarter notes in that particular line. Begin playing immediately after the clicks.

GETTING STARTED HOW TO READ MUSIC

Why read music? There *are* talented drummers who do not read music. The late big-band drummer Buddy Rich was one of them. He listened to his band play an arrangement once or twice, then sat down and pretty much had it figured out. (His talent and ability to memorize was exceptional!) All drummers learn to a significant degree about playing by watching and listening.

For purposes of learning from a book, it is necessary to communicate ideas through written music. Learning this language, like any language, takes a little effort and practice. **The advantage is that you will have an added skill that others may not**. If you wish to play beyond your own enjoyment—in a band, for example—you will be a step ahead of others. You will have basic music reading skills, which will be an advantage when communicating with other musicians who also read music or in getting work!

MINI MUSIC LESSON SYMBOLS FOR SOUNDS—NOTES

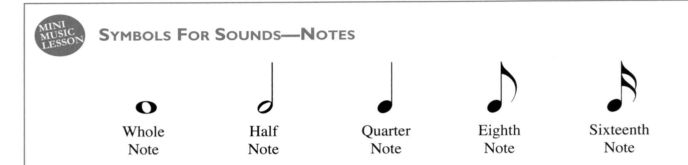

| Whole Note | Half Note | Quarter Note | Eighth Note | Sixteenth Note |

Each of the above characters symbolizes sound. The difference between them is duration, or length. A half note is half the length of a whole note, a quarter is one-quarter the length of a whole, an eighth is one-eighth of a whole, etc.—that is why they are named as such.

SYMBOLS FOR SILENCE—RESTS

| Whole Rest | Half Rest | Quarter Rest | Eighth Rest | Sixteenth Rest |

Each of the above characters, called rests, symbolizes silence. In terms of length or duration, they correspond to the notes. A whole rest is equal in length to a whole note, a half note equal to a half rest, and so on.

Simply speaking, all music is composed of these two types of symbols: notes and rests (or sound and silence). These are the symbols you actually read as you play written music.

GETTING
STARTED THE FRAMEWORK

In order to make music, it is necessary to place notes and rests on a type of roadmap. We call this roadmap the staff. The **staff** consists of five horizontal lines.

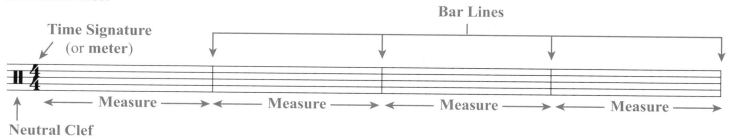

The vertical lines which divide the staff into sections are **bar lines**. The divided sections are known as **measures** or **bars**. The two short vertical lines at the very beginning form the **neutral clef** used for non-pitched music and needs no further explanation here. The stacked numbers at the beginning of the staff are the **time signature**, sometimes called **meter**. (NOTE: Below, **double bar lines** are used before each change in meter.)

The time signature is of special significance. The *top number* represents the number of beats in one measure (in this case, 4 beats per measure). The *bottom number* indicates the type of note or rest that will get one beat. In this case, 4 = a quarter note or rest. If the bottom number were an 8, it would signify an eighth note or rest; if it were a 2, it would mean a half note or rest, etc.

Various Time Signatures:

How many beats?

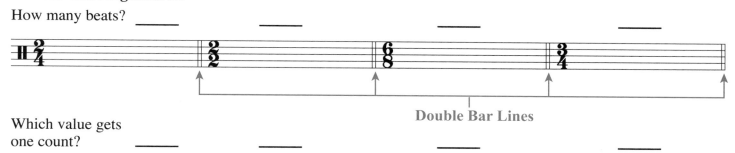

Which value gets one count?

For each of the above time signatures, how many beats are there in each bar? What note or rest value gets one count? (Review the third paragraph on this page if there is any question in your mind.) After you're sure of the answers, check them at the bottom of this page.

In order to better understand the concept of a time signature, let's look at some simple examples of music on the next page.

Answers: $\frac{2}{4}$—2 beats per bar, quarter note or rest gets 1 count; $\frac{2}{2}$—per bar, half note or rest gets 1 count; $\frac{6}{8}$ 6 beats per bar, eighth note or rest gets 1 count; $\frac{3}{4}$—3 beats per bar, quarter note or rest gets 1 count.

CD Tracks 34–37

GETTING STARTED — READING YOUR FIRST LINES OF MUSIC

In Ex. 1, there are 4 beats in each measure. There can be 4 quarter rests, 4 quarter notes or combinations of quarter notes and rests—but there can only be 4 types of quarter configurations total. The next line of music (Ex. 2) includes 3 quarter notes or rests in each bar. The third example (Ex. 3) is made up of 2 quarter notes or rests per bar.

Count evenly aloud ("one…two…three…four…one…two…three…four…") as indicated above Ex. 1. As you count, tap on your snare drum when there is a note below the number; do nothing (except continue counting) when there is a rest. Try it several times until you feel at least somewhat comfortable.

Quarter Notes (sound) **Quarter Rests** (silence)

Ending double bar indicates end of music or music section

Try the next line (Ex. 2). This time you'll be counting in patterns of three, tapping on your snare each time a quarter note appears below. Again, do this several times until you get the hang of it.

The third line (Ex. 3) is a bit different because you rest on the first count. Also, notice that this line has six measures, rather than four.

The last line (Ex. 4) is also a bit tricky, but should be fun. Like the first line, you'll be counting in four again.

DAILY WORKOUT #1

A. Carefully review the instructions back on pages 12–15 for developing your wrists and fingers. Work on Technique Builder #1 on page 15.

B. Work on the counting exercises above (Ex. 1–4). Try to look only at the music, rather than at the counting numbers above the notes.

PRACTICE TIP

For Daily Workout #1 A, you should strive for relaxation. It may take several days until you start feeling comfortable. When working on B, remember to count steadily and evenly. If it is difficult, try counting more slowly. Patience will always be a virtue as you practice … and the rewards will be great!

THE LINES & SPACES— WHERE INSTRUMENTS ARE INDICATED

GETTING STARTED

The purpose in having lines and spaces on the staff in drum music is to indicate which instruments to play. (Pitched instruments, such as a guitar or piano, use the lines and spaces to determine what pitches to play.) The following shows where each instrument on your drumset is placed on the staff:

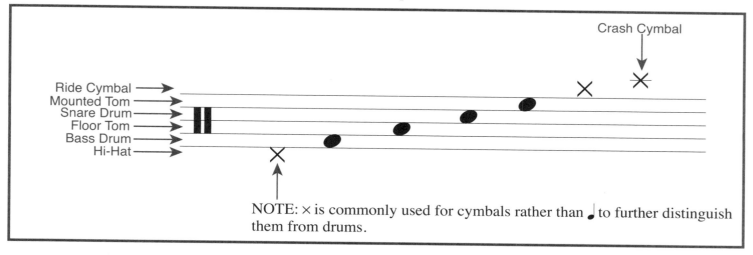

NOTE: ✕ is commonly used for cymbals rather than ♩ to further distinguish them from drums.

READING THE LINES & SPACES

In the following exercises you will be playing all the instruments on your set. It will take some time to get used to which instrument to play. At first, the instruments are marked in parenthesis. Use whichever hand seems most natural. (All the hi-hat and bass drum notes should be played with the foot unless otherwise indicated.)

USING YOUR FEET

Surprisingly, there are different ways to approach playing with your feet. The technique you use may influence how you adjust your throne.

FLAT TECHNIQUE

The foot lies flat on the pedal at all times. In a resting position, the hi-hat is open or the bass drum beater "cocked" away from the head. To play, pressure is applied to the entire foot. In the case of the bass drum, it is preferable to allow the beater to return to the cocked position immediately after striking the head.

TOE TECHNIQUE

In a resting position, pressure is applied to the pedal with the toe end of the foot—the hi-hat remains closed; the bass drum beater rests against the head. The heel doesn't touch the pedal. To play, the entire leg lifts slightly, bouncing on the ball of the foot. Many drummers who use this have their throne adjusted a little higher. This technique is especially useful when playing faster rhythms. Also, this can produce more power and, therefore, is the common choice of rock drummers.

HEEL & TOE ("ROCKING") TECHNIQUE

This is usually associated with the hi-hat. As the name implies, the foot rocks back and forth. First, the toe end of the foot presses into the pedal and the heel comes off the pedal. Then, the heel comes down as the toe end of the foot rises, so the foot actually moves like the base of a rocking chair. This technique, while not useful for fast music, is very comfortable for keeping an even pace for other, not-so-fast tunes, especially moderate jazz (swing).

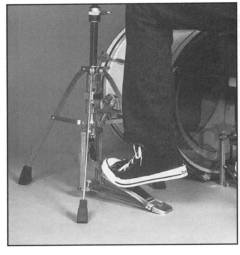
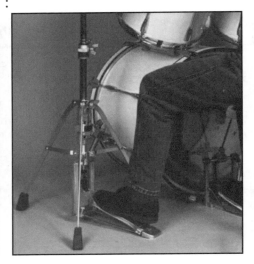

CHOOSING A TECHNIQUE

As with choosing grips, there is no right or wrong pedal technique. The flat technique utilizes economy of motion in the case of the bass drum because the beater doesn't have to be brought back in a position ready to strike—it is already there. But there are players—many of whom are "rockers"—who swear by the toe technique. You may want to try each for a while, then go with what you prefer. Or you may wish to use both or a sort of hybrid.

Try the following exercises using the three techniques mentioned above. Play them several times until you feel somewhat comfortable with each.

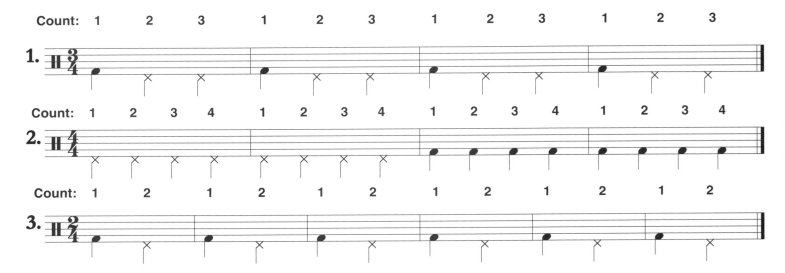

 WHERE TO PLAY

WITH THE STICK

There are a few areas of the stick that are commonly referred to in other books, magazines and elsewhere. While the vast majority of playing is done with the tip, the shoulder and the butt of the stick are sometimes used.

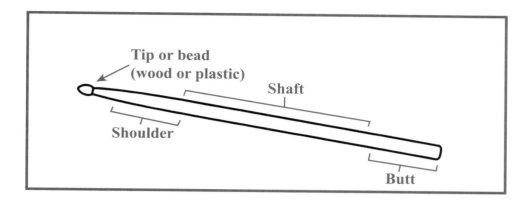

Tip or bead (wood or plastic)

Shaft

Shoulder

Butt

ON THE DRUMHEAD

Depending upon where you strike the drumhead, you can produce different sounds. Playing near the rim produces a thin, high-pitched sound; playing at the center produces a full-bodied sound. Ordinarily, drummers play slightly off center, about an inch or two. But don't forget that different sounds are valuable assets that will enable you to create the unique "feel" and sound character you're looking for by mixing various tone colors in your playing.

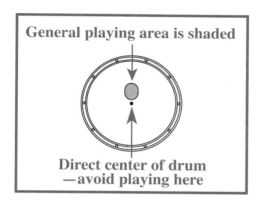

General playing area is shaded

Direct center of drum
—avoid playing here

ON THE CYMBAL

The parts of the cymbal are few, but the areas upon which to play are many. Some progressive drummers even utilize the edge in a special manner—by striking it with the stick perpendicular (at a 90-degree angle).

Generally, the ride cymbal is played with the tip of the stick about 2 inches from the edge.

The shoulder of the drum stick may be used for accents or contrast, playing on the shoulder, edge or bell.

The crash cymbal is most often played with a glancing blow across the edge of the cymbal with the shoulder of the stick. However, you may find other techniques and playing areas, as with the ride cymbal, that provide sounds you'll want to use.

Never be afraid to experiment and try unusual ideas.

Playing on the bell of a cymbal creates a "ping" sound somewhat like a high-pitched cowbell. As a result, it is used in Latin and African rhythms, but also as a driving pulse in rock when played with the shoulder or butt end of the stick. (When practicing exercises you can try playing on the bell of the cymbal to achieve a different effect.)

Try to identify the bell sound in recordings, making note of how it is used within the music and the effect it creates.

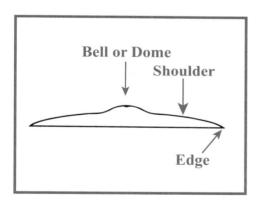

Bell or Dome

Shoulder

Edge

PART II Learning the Basics

THE PACE OF MUSIC—TEMPO

 The staff serves as a kind of road map to read music. The goal is to get from one place to another—in this case, from the beginning of the music to the end. As explained, we first must look at the time signature before we begin to know how many beats are in a measure and what kind of note or rest gets one beat.

Then, as we begin the journey, we travel at an even pace. This pace is known as **tempo**. It is the pulse or beat of music. When an audience claps along to music at a concert, they are naturally feeling the beat or tempo. You probably have found yourself tapping your foot many times to music you enjoy.

Before you begin playing any music, you must have the tempo in mind. This is why a musician counts to other musicians before beginning to play. In this manner, everyone knows the tempo before the music starts. The drummer is always in charge of maintaining a steady, even tempo, though it is also the responsibility of the other musicians. For this reason, the drummer is often called the "time keeper." (More about this later.)

FINDING THE RIGHT TEMPO— THE METRONOME

There is a device that should be used to determine tempos: a **metronome**. It indicates tempo by a click or a beep and some models also have a blinking light. Metronomes are available at all music dealers and are a *must* for serious musicians! There are a wide variety from which to choose, including mechanical (which are wound up) and electronic. Models with the blinking or flashing light are definitely helpful for drummers because of the sound factor. Those with an earphone may also be desirable. There are also metronome apps available.

For most exercises in this book, there will be a metronome marking. It consists of a note equaling a number (for example, ♩ = 96) and appears just above the time signature. Simply set your metronome to the number and turn it on. This will be the tempo (as in the example, a quarter note will equal 96 beats per minute). In most instances, you will be given a range of numbers from which to choose (i.e., 60–72). It is a good idea to try a slower tempo first (the smaller number) and work up slowly to a faster one. *However, don't hesitate to choose a tempo slower than what is marked!*

GET INTO THE GROOVE

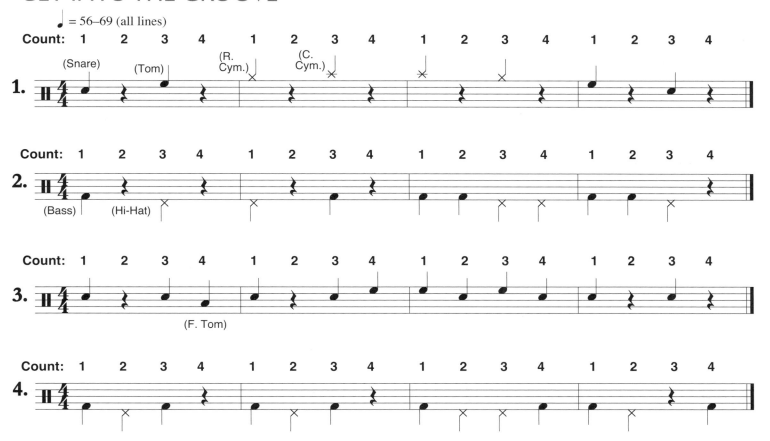

In the next example, always play the ride cymbal with your right hand and the drums with your left

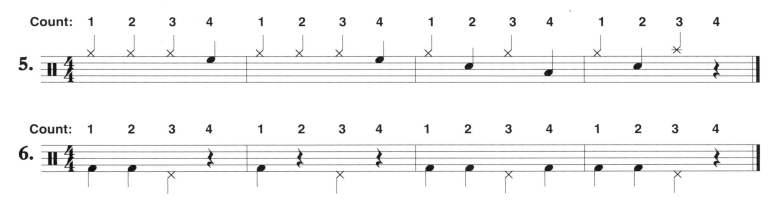

DAILY WORKOUT #2

A. Play the above exercises four times. Increase the tempo slightly each day until you can play ♩ = 69 without much difficulty.

B. Play along with some of your favorite recordings, keeping the beat with one hand on a cymbal or drum. Listen to the tempo carefully and try to keep the beat steady. You should try this a few times playing only the bass drum and then only the hi-hat.

C. Continue to work on Technique Builder #1 (page 15).

PRACTICE TIP The idea behind A is to become familiar with the lines and spaces, as well as with counting aloud. Calling out numbers while playing is an important facet of learning rhythms and reading. Approach B as a fun exercise, but really concentrate on the tempo. You should never fall behind or get ahead of the beat!

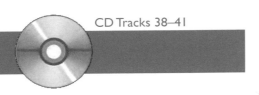

CD Tracks 38–41

ROCKIN', REELIN', READIN' AND REPEATIN'

The purpose of these next two pages is to gain more skill at reading music—particularly in getting used to where the instruments appear on the staff. (These exercises won't sound much like drum beats.) Don't become frustrated if this takes a little practice. In time, reading music becomes second nature, much like reading the words in this sentence.

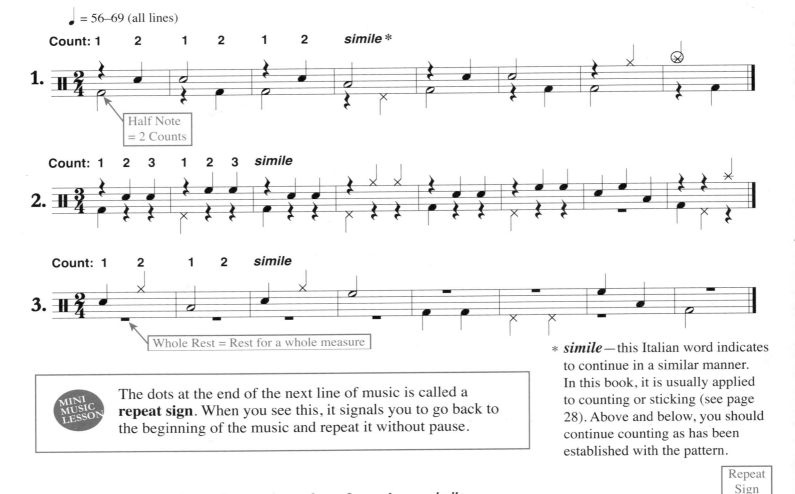

Half Note = 2 Counts

Whole Rest = Rest for a whole measure

> **MINI MUSIC LESSON**
> The dots at the end of the next line of music is called a **repeat sign**. When you see this, it signals you to go back to the beginning of the music and repeat it without pause.

* **simile**—this Italian word indicates to continue in a similar manner. In this book, it is usually applied to counting or sticking (see page 28). Above and below, you should continue counting as has been established with the pattern.

Repeat Sign

Did you see the repeat sign at the end of line 4 and remember to repeat the music?

DAILY WORKOUT #3

A. Play all music on the previous page and on this one. If you don't feel comfortable with this workout after a week of practicing, spend a few more days before going on to the next page.

B. As on the last workout, play along with any recordings or the radio, keeping the beat on a cymbal or drum.

C. Continue to work on Technique Builder # 1 on page 15.

MIXIN' IT UP

Here is further reading practice with whole, half and quarter notes and rests. Always count aloud and watch the time signatures. Also, look for lines which have repeat signs at the end!

Whole Note = 4 Counts

A. Play the above exercises four times. You may wish to start at a tempo slightly slower than ♩ = 56 at first. Gradually increase the tempo when you play a line without mistakes or hesitation until you reach ♩ = 69.

B. Practice the three basic beats from "Play Now!" on the play-along cassette, or continue B from page 26.

PRACTICE TIP...... Be sure you are observing the repeat sign (when it appears) without losing the tempo. Your metronome will let you know if you are falling behind or getting ahead of the beat.

CD Tracks 42–45

IT TAKES TWO

Whoever said you can't do two things at once? Drummers often play *four* things at one time!

In order to build to that stage, let's try playing two notes at the same time. Often, the measures in each line are the same with an occasional change. Take it slowly at first and always remember to count as you play. This time the counting is not marked on the page. (If you feel you need it, you can pencil it in above the music. First try counting without marking it, then only mark it where it's needed.) In place of the counting is **sticking**. This indicates which stick to use. An "R" above a note means to play with the right hand; an "L" signifies the left. Try to follow the sticking as you read the music. The stickings marked are only suggestions and are not set in stone.

Prime Time

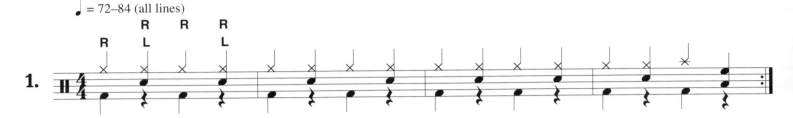

Cool Waltz

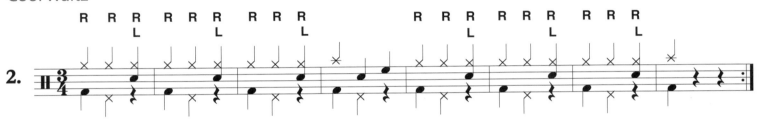

Hail to the Chief (March)

Slavic Backbeat

DAILY WORKOUT #5

A. Practice this page with a metronome. The goal is to be able to play all four lines at ♩ = 84 while remaining relaxed and keeping an even tempo at all times.

B. Listen to some of your favorite recordings. Can you play any of the lines above along with them? Are any of the recordings in ¾ time? Whenever you listen to music, see if you can tell what the **meter** (another name for time signature) is for that music.

PRACTICE TIP If you have difficulty with this page of music, try only the feet, then the hands. Then try various combinations of one hand and one foot. Finally, play it all together as written. This is a practice tip that you should use often in this book.

STICK TO IT!

These easy patterns should be fun. As always, counting helps you correctly place the notes and keep a steady tempo.

Swing It!

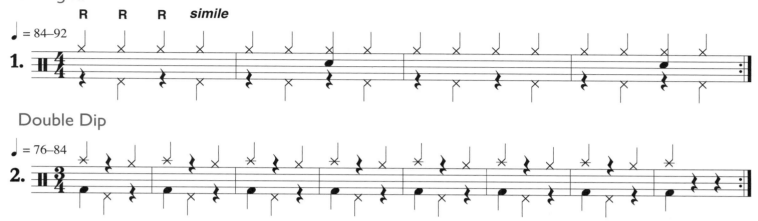

Double Dip

This next example may require extra effort. After completing the first line, continue without pause to the next line, then the same at the end of the second line (as if the three lines were one long line of music). In music, the single bar at the end of a line indicates to go on to the next line.

Rock Solid

Technique ...Builder... 2 To practice facility in moving about your set, as well as in developing coordination, play the; following exercise. Start slowly and very gradually pick up speed. As soon as you feel the least bit of tension in any muscles, begin to gradually slow down. Repeat this four times. The trick is to stay relaxed while keeping the notes evenly spaced!

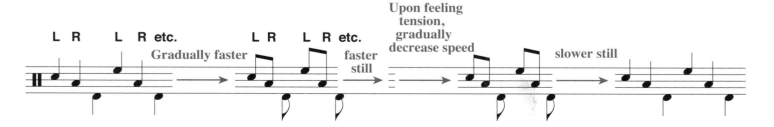

CRAZY EIGHTHS

Up until now, you've been counting on the beat ("one…two…three…" and so forth). Here, you'll learn to count between the quarter-note beats.

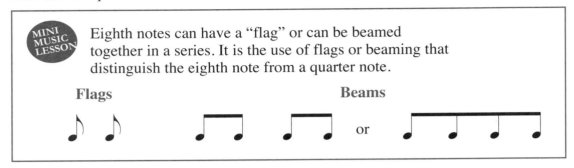

MINI MUSIC LESSON Eighth notes can have a "flag" or can be beamed together in a series. It is the use of flags or beaming that distinguish the eighth note from a quarter note.

Flags

Beams

A measure of eighth notes in 4/4 time appears like this:

Count them as indicated above ("+" is spoken as "and"). Now set your metronome to the tempo indicated. Count again aloud as your metronome clicks. You must fit the "ands" evenly between the beats, making it sound smooth.

Try the following line on your set. Count aloud as you play, alternating hands (right, left, right, etc). The bass drum keeps the beat, like a metronome would.

Notice that in the last bar, there is no need to count "and" after beats three and four. (But you should still leave the correct spacing between those last two beats as if you were counting "and.")

An eighth rest looks like this: ♪

Try counting, then playing, the following lines, which combines eighth notes and rests. The rhythms can be tricky, so count carefully.

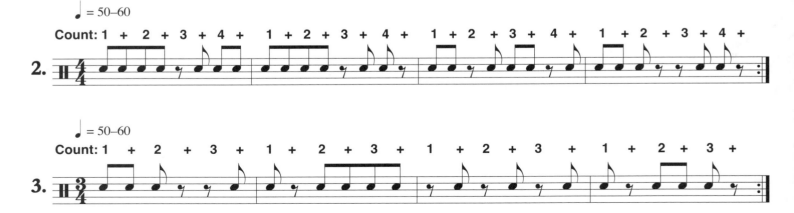

MORE EIGHTHS

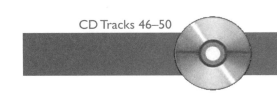

CD Tracks 46–50

This page will give you more experience playing eighth notes while becoming accustomed to "moving around the set." This will assist you in learning to play fills a bit later. The feet play the same pattern in each measure, so you can concentrate on the eighth notes in the hands. Use your metronome. Since stickings are not marked, find stickings that seem naturally comfortable. If you wish, you can jot in the stickings you like for reference when you practice.

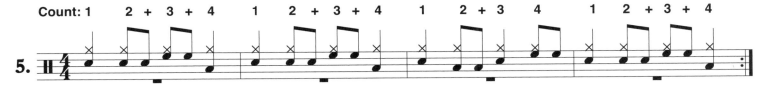

This last line uses only hands. The right hand stays with the ride cymbal, while the left plays the drums.

Did you remember to repeat as marked?

A. Count aloud, then count and play all lines on the previous page. Try it with and without a metronome (♩ = 60).

B. Practice this page with a metronome. Gradually work up to ♩ = 72.

PRACTICE TIP It is sometimes said that if you can't count it, you can't play it. This is true! As with the previous workout, if you have difficulty with any of the above, try only the feet, then only hands, finally putting it all together.

LOOK MA, NO HANDS!

Here are some exercises to help develop technique for your feet. You may wish to review page 22, which discusses the various techniques for the bass drum and hi-hat.

Use only the toe technique on hi-hat for this line.

A. Practice this page with a metronome. Gradually work up to ♩ = 80.

B. Work on Technique Builder #3.

PRACTICE TIP Try the assorted techniques described on page 22 for the exercises. Determine which technique feels most comfortable for each line, then practice using that particular technique.

KEEPING TIME

Many of the exercises from here on will consist of the repetition of a measure. The repetition of a stylistic pattern (while not necessarily an exact repetition) is known as playing **time**. Some drummers, such as the late big-band drummer Mel Lewis and rocker Charlie Watts (The Rolling Stones), have been known for their ability to "keep great time," rather than using flashy technique. What this really means is that they keep a steady beat and everything they play fits together and sounds appropriate within the context of the music. *Keeping great time is something every drummer should strive for!*

In the exercises below, concentrate by *listening* to your playing. These exercises are kept somewhat simple to enable you to do this.

 The next exercise is 16 measures. Music often consists of 4-, 8-, 12- and 16-bar **phrases** (small sections of music). This piece actually consists of four groups of four-bar phrases. Line 3 on page 29 is constructed the same way.

CD Track 51

Play the ride cymbal pattern on closed hi-hat throughout.

EASY DOES IT

You will now learn to play time (patterns) for a few basic styles of music. As you go through this book, you will encounter more patterns for the various styles ... and they will become more interesting and exciting as your skills develop.

The counting is not marked, but you should still count whenever you have trouble with a measure. The stickings are not marked either, so you may want to pencil in stickings. (The right hand always plays the ride cymbal.)

 MINI MUSIC LESSON When a measure is to be played exactly as the one before it, a sign is used indicating this called a **one-bar repeat sign**: %

Play the first measure, then play it again as indicated by the repeat sign.

Waltz

♩ = 84–104 (all lines)

1.

Rock

2.

Polka

3.

Reggae

4.

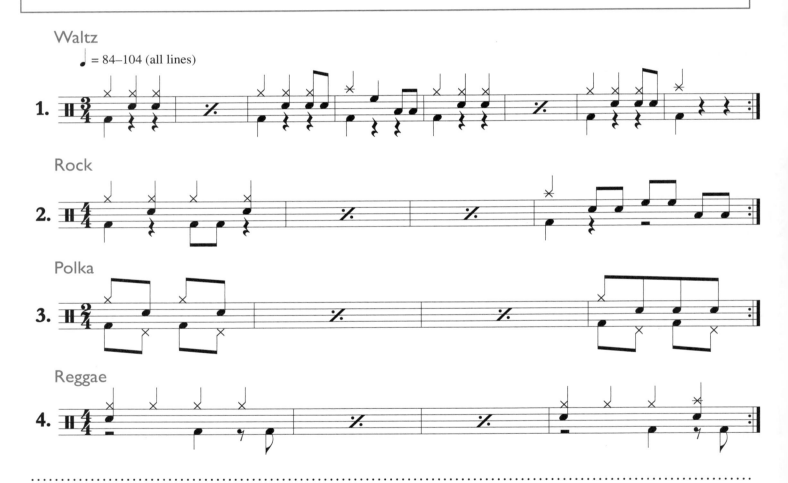

Technique ...Builder... 3 INTRODUCTION TO THE DOUBLE-STROKE ROLL

The following exercise is like the previous Technique Builder. The first stroke is executed with the wrist and the second is a bounce controlled by the fingers. The goal is to make both strokes equal in volume. Start slowly, then gradually get faster (always keeping the notes even), then start slowing down when you've reached top speed without your muscles tensing up.

R R L L etc.   R R L L   etc.
Gradually faster   faster still

Upon feeling tension, gradually decrease speed

slower still

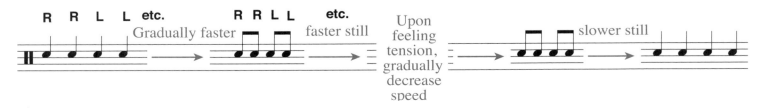

THREE'S COMPANY

You should be ready to progress to playing three notes at one time. This really opens up the possibilities. Again, it is wise to first practice the feet separately, then the hands, combining them afterwards. These exercises are similar to the previous page to help make it easy for you.

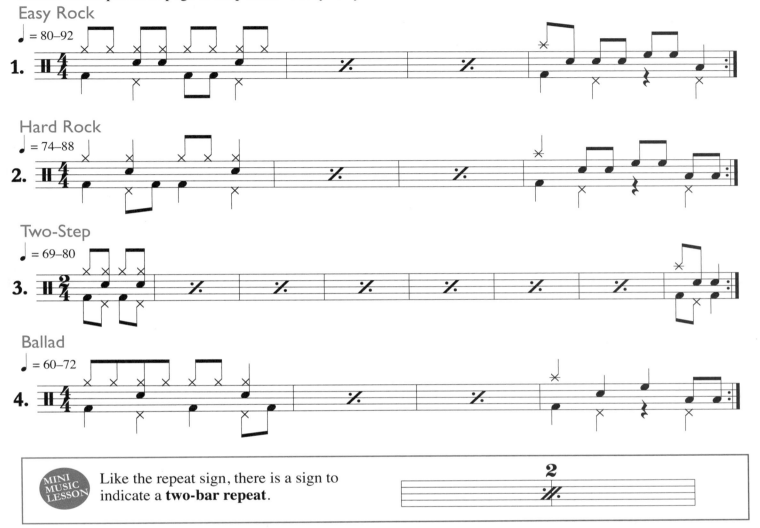

Play the first two bars, then at the two-bar repeat, play the two bars again without pause.

A. Practice this page along with the previous one. Try not using a metronome, except if you wish to find the tempo.

B. Instead of the ride cymbal, experiment by playing the ride-cymbal pattern on closed hi-hat. (Don't play the written hi-hat part in this situation.)

C. Work on Technique Builder #3.

PRACTICE TIP...... If you ever wish to practice, but do not have access to your set, (perhaps because others are sleeping) try playing an imaginary set. In a similar fashion to those who jokingly play "air guitar," drummers often can practice coordination of feet and hands in any space. It doesn't feel exactly the same, but it comes close enough to help with coordination. If practical, a set of pillows will work in place of practice pads to drum upon with sticks.

FILL IN THE BLANKS

You may recall from page 34 that music is often composed of phrases (small 4-, 8- or 16-bar sections). Additionally, you might have noticed that many of the lines you've practiced on the last few pages consist of a pattern and, at the end of the line, there is a distinct change from that pattern. This change of pattern is a **fill**. It is a drummer *filling* in a sort of "hole" in the music. Ordinarily this hole occurs at the end of a musical phrase (and other instruments may be filling it up in addition to or instead of the drummer).

The following lines have fills written at the end of the four-bar phrases. Feel free to create your own fills and write them in the blank measure. Your fill may replace the one that is written.

This last exercise utilizes a special technique with the snare drum. The stick is flipped over with the tip or bead keeping contact with the drumhead. The butt end of the stick is raised and brought down to strike the rim.

This technique is sometimes known as a **cross-stick rim shot**. This technique is often used in country, Latin and jazz music.

Basic Bossa

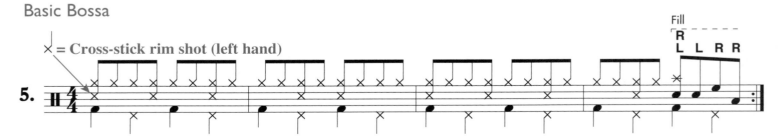

More Basics

This section continues with the fundamentals of music, drumming technique and various exercises. However, this section moves quickly, so it may take more time to progress through the pages. The key is to *practice carefully*.

Study each page, avoiding the temptation to rush through them. These concepts will require extra effort, so be patient. Above all, do not move ahead to this section unless you feel you've mastered previous pages. Now is a good time to pick out those pages which gave you a bit of trouble and review them for a while. Believe me, it will payoff in the long-run.

NOTE & REST REVIEW

To better understand music notation and the length or duration of notes and rests, the relationship between them should be clear. (You may first wish to review page 18 and the names of the rests and notes). Remember that for every type of note, there exists a rest of equal length.

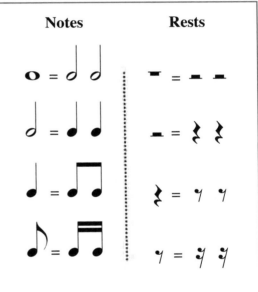

One whole note or rest equals two halves:

One half note or rest equals two quarters:

One quarter note or rest equals two eighths:

One eighth note or rest equals two sixteenths (discussed on the following page):

Here's another way to look at the relationships of notes:

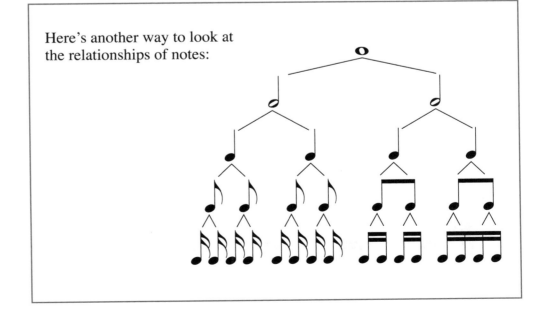

SWEET SIXTEENTHS

In order to learn more advanced patterns and fills, it will be necessary to add sixteenth notes and rests to your vocabulary.

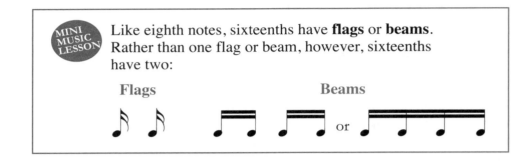

Like eighth notes, sixteenths have **flags** or **beams**. Rather than one flag or beam, however, sixteenths have two:

A measure of sixteenth notes in various meters follows:

Count as indicated above, then set your metronome to the tempo indicated. Count again aloud as your metronome clicks. You must fit the "e" and "ah" evenly between the eighth beats, making it sound smooth.

Try the following line on your set. Count aloud as you play, alternating hands. The bass drum keeps the beat, like a metronome would.

A sixteenth rest looks like this: ♪

Try counting, then playing the following line which combines sixteenth notes and rests:

MORE SIXTEENTHS

Here are more exercises to practice reading sixteenth notes and rests. Be sure to count to become accustomed to these. This is going to take extra time. Note how eighth notes are often beamed to sixteenths. Beams tie together notes within a beat so each beat is visually distinct.

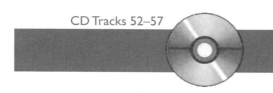

CD Tracks 52–57

Though counting is not marked, you should be able to count the next lines.

DAILY WORKOUT #9

A. Review page 36. Create sixteenth-note fills for that page.

B. Practice lines 1–4 on different drums (as in lines 5 and 6). Also try this for lines 1 and 2 on the previous page.

C. Continue work on Technique Builder #3.

PRACTICE TIP Many musicians have a tendency to rush sixteenth notes because they are thought of as fast. Practice with a metronome to be sure you do not get into this bad habit.

CD Tracks 58–62

DOTTED RHYTHMS

MINI MUSIC LESSON

When a note or rest is followed by a dot, it increases its value by one half. Here are the most frequent dotted-note values you'll come across:

$\begin{array}{lll} \textrm{♩.} & \textrm{or} & = 3 \textrm{ quarters} \\ \textrm{♪.} & \textrm{or} & = 3 \textrm{ eighths} \\ \textrm{♪.} & \textrm{or} & = 3 \textrm{ sixteenths} \end{array}$

A dot may be applied to *any* note or rest (in addition to those shown above).

Try reading, then practicing, the following lines:

♩ = 64–72 (all lines)

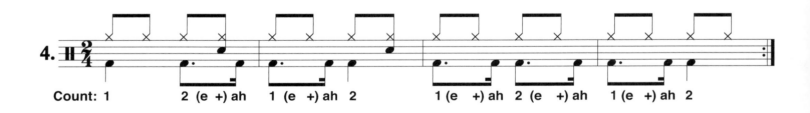

DYNAMICS—WAKING UP THE MUSIC

An element of all music that creates interest is contrast—variations in the music, sometimes subtle, by way of volume, types of sounds (playing on different cymbals and drums), tempo, etc.

Let's examine volume. Pick one of your favorite exercises on the previous page. Try playing it as softly as possible the first time, then play loudly when you repeat it. Here are symbols used in music to indicate the amount of volume to be used. These indications (derived from the Italian language) are known as **dynamics**.

Symbol	Italian	English
pp	*pianissimo*	very soft
p	*piano*	soft
mp	*mezzo piano*	medium soft
mf	*mezzo forte*	medium loud
f	*forte*	loud
ff	*fortissimo*	very loud
◁	*crescendo*	gradually louder
▷	*decrecendo*	gradually softer

There is an additional type of dynamic called an **accent**. This symbol, which resembles a "greater than" sign in math, appears above or below a note.

Notes with accents are played a bit louder than others, usually by one or two dynamic levels. Try this easy exercise.

Accents—Play marked notes *f* (loud), one dynamic louder than *mf*.

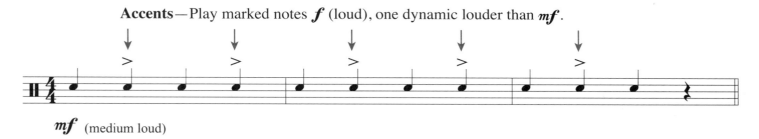

mf (medium loud)

Remember, *an accent only affects the note that is marked.*

An accent may not always mean "loud." Play this exercise.

pp (very soft)

Since this exercise is marked *pp* (very soft), the accented notes are played louder, but should only be *p* (soft) or, at the loudest, *mp* (medium soft).

Accents are used on the next page and throughout the rest of the book. Keep an eye out for them. Like other dynamics, they help bring life to music.

DIGGING IN!

Here are some basic rock-oriented patterns using sixteenths and dotted rhythms. Fills are played in the fourth bar. *The right hand plays* *on a closed hi-hat, read from the ride-cymbal line.* (Because of this, the hi-hat has been omitted here.) These are tricky, so it may take extra effort until you feel comfortable with them. Also, watch for dynamic markings (see the previous page).

A. Practice page 40 and this page. Create and write in your own dynamics for page 40.

B. Try leaving the hi-hat a little open in lines 3 & 4.

PRACTICE TIP Before playing each line, look over the final measure carefully. This should help you play each line smoothly without stumbling over the change in pattern at the end of each line. Glancing over music, searching for trouble spots and counting them out before reading them, is a good habit to make.

HI-HAT TECHNIQUE

Up to this point, all playing on the hi-hat has been with it closed or partially open. It is common to play rhythms on the hi-hat while intermittently opening and closing it. The standard symbol for indicating open hi-hat is ○ and closed is **+**.

Try playing these lines. (The hi-hat is written where the ride cymbal is usually indicated.) The hi-hat need not be opened fully. In fact, this is rarely done. The cymbals only need to be slightly separated in order to create the desired "sizzle" sound.

The degree to which you open the hi-hat depends on the sound you're looking for. Like other aspects of drumming, don't resist experimentation!

A. After practicing the page as written, create fills in the fourth bars of each line.

B. Experiment opening and closing the hi-hat with lines 1, 2 and 5 on the previous page.

C. Continue work on Technique Builder #3.

PRACTICE TIP A common problem with hi-hat technique is coordinating both feet. As a result, it may be very helpful to practice only bass drum and hi-hat without using hands, then adding your hands afterwards.

ROLLS

A guitar, trumpet or other instrument can sustain or hold a note. But how does a drummer sustain a sound on a drum? The answer is by playing a **roll**. There are several types of rolls:

Single Stroke

This roll sounds less like a constant, sustained sound and more like fast individual notes. It is often used on low toms and cymbals to sustain sound. Technique Builder #1 on page 15 showed how this is executed. The roll may be implemented in fills and solos.

Double Stroke

This roll can produce a good sustained sound when played "closed" (fast), but also can resemble the single stroke when played "open" (slow). It is mostly used on the snare and also, to a lesser extent, on the toms, closed hi-hat and cymbals. Technique Builder #3 on page 35 introduced this roll. The ability to play this roll is especially useful in jazz drumming, but is applicable in all styles.

Multiple Bounce (sometimes referred to as "buzz," crushed, unmeasured or orchestral roll)

The concept behind this roll is to get many bounces per stick stroke. The bounces are not controlled the way they are with the double-stroke roll. On the drumset, its use is a bit limited. Technique Builder #4 on the next page will instruct you in how to play this roll.

NOTATION

A roll is designated in music by one of two ways:

1) Three diagonal slashes above the note or a combination of slashes and flags equaling three in number (cutting across the stem when there is one).

2) Multiple bounce only—a "z" above the note, cutting across the stem. This notation is rare.

As you can see, the roll is often tied to a note (with a curved line) to indicate on which beat the roll should end.

ROLLIN' OVER

CD Tracks 63–67

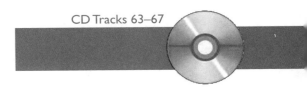

Here are some exercises for the snare drum. Try either the double-stroke or multiple-bounce roll after you've become familiar with Technique Builder #4 at the bottom of this page.

....

 **Technique ...Builder... 4 INTRODUCTION TO THE MULTIPLE-BOUNCE ROLL**

To learn this roll, first press the stick into the head loosely enough so there are many rapid bounces. There should be almost no space between each bounce, and it should resemble a "buzz" sound. Do this with each hand.

After practicing this fundamental technique for a few minutes, try the exercise. You should play the "buzz" stroke, alternating hands, attempting to make smooth connections between each stroke.

This is how the roll is played. Continue practicing this, striving to achieve a constant, seamless sound.

TRIPLETS

In the context of one beat, you've played two notes (eighths), and
four notes (sixteenths), evenly.

Eighths

Two notes per beat (eighth notes):

Sixteenths

Four notes per beat (sixteenth notes):

Now, we will learn three notes per
beat—**triplets**. A triplet is a group
of three notes played in place of
two notes of the same value. Play
the following exercise, using the

bass drum to keep the beat. Keep
the space between the notes even as
with eighths and sixteenths.

Eighth-note Triplets

Three notes per beat:

Triplets are indicated by a "*3*"
above or below the note grouping.
The above example utilized eighth-
note triplets, but they may exist as
quarter-note and sixteenth-notes
and other groupings.

To play quarter-note triplets, first
think of eighth-note triplets, but
play every other one. The following
exercise, in which every other note
is accented in the first bar, will help
you get the feel for the quarter-note
triplets in the second bar:

> Brackets are used to indicate groupings
> where notes are not beamed.

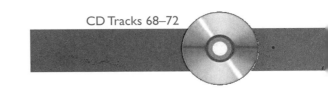

MORE TRIPLETS

These exercises should help you become more familiar with triplets.

You may play the bass drum part on the hi-hat for variety. Don't overlook dynamics!

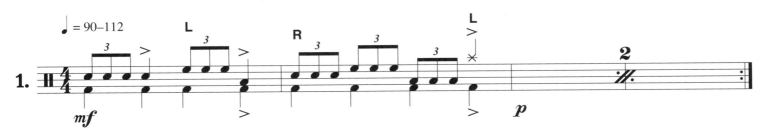

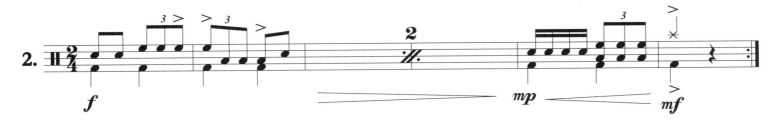

DAILY WORKOUT #12

A. Review all roll exercises on page 45. Try playing each line on various drums, using a single-stroke roll when playing on the floor tom.

B. Practice the three lines on page 46, along with those on this page. Strive to make all triplets even.

PRACTICE TIP

With A, *be patient*! Even those who've been playing for years continue to work on perfecting rolls. Spend extra practice time with rolls and they will gradually improve.

PICK-UPS

In all the music you've played in this book, you've begun on beat 1 (or "on the downbeat," as they say). But music doesn't always start on the downbeat. When this occurs, the music is described as having "pick-ups."

When repeating these lines, include the pick-up.

Whatever is missing from the pick-up measure is sometimes found in the last measure. In other words, the first and last "incomplete" measures in a piece together make a complete one. This way of writing music is an old practice that is sometimes still observed. (Don't let it confuse you!)

In the next line, there is a double bar. Do not play the pick-up when you repeat the line. Go to the double bar, which has a repeat sign to indicate where the repeat begins.

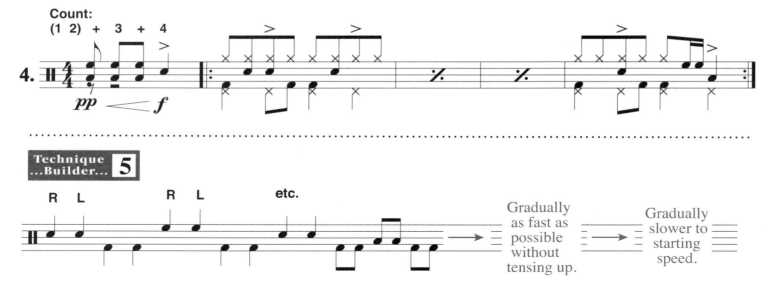

Technique ...Builder... 5

FIRST AND SECOND ENDINGS

MINI MUSIC LESSON

Look at line 1. Notice the indications at the end of the line. These are referred to as **first** and **second endings**. Play the line all the way to the repeat sign (at the first ending), repeat as you normally would, but when you reach…

The First Ending　　　| 1.

…the second time, do not play the music under it. Skip it and play the music under:

The Second Ending　　　| 2.

To help focus on understanding first and second endings, the following lines are similar to the beats played on the previous page.

♩ = 8–112 (all lines)

DAILY WORKOUT #13

A. Play the exercises on pages 48 and 49 as written, then play the ride cymbal part on hi-hat employing open and closed techniques discussed on page 43.

B. Practice Technique Builder #5 .

C. Continue developing rolls (pages 44 and 45), and review triplet exercises on page 47.

PRACTICE TIP

When reading music, the trick is to look ahead while playing. This becomes especially necessary when repeating phrases. Before finishing the measure indicating to repeat, your eyes should already have located the measure where the repeat begins.

CD Tracks 73–77

NEW METERS

Some time signatures are based on groupings of three eighth notes. Since we have learned triplets (which is a grouping of three), these meters should be relatively easy to understand.

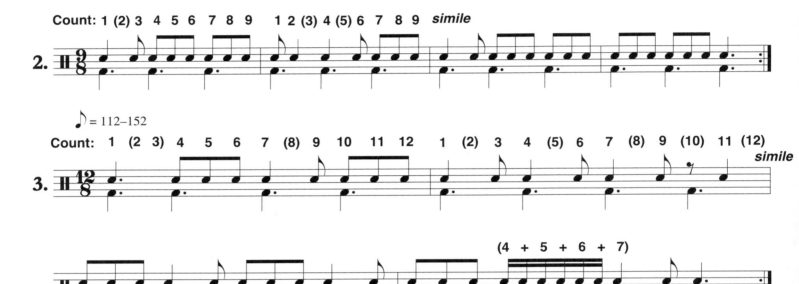

These three examples may be counted in another manner, particularly when played at quicker tempos. Rather than counting in 6, the first $\frac{6}{8}$ example may be thought of "in 2." The bass drum plays on beats 1 and 4, but may feel more like "1" and "2" as in $\frac{2}{4}$ time. The $\frac{9}{8}$ example may be felt more "in 3" ($\frac{3}{4}$ time) and $\frac{12}{8}$ "in 4" ($\frac{4}{4}$ time).

Here is one other meter you haven't seen. If you recall the discussion on page 18, in line 4 there are two beats per measure and the half note gets one count for this particular time signature. Line 5 has the symbol ₵ (referred to as "cut time"), which is exactly the same time signature as $\frac{2}{2}$.

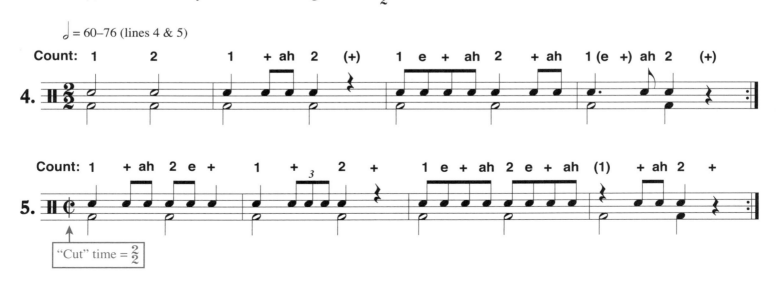

"Cut" time = $\frac{2}{2}$

BASIC BEATS USING NEW METERS

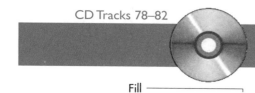
CD Tracks 78–82

Here are basic patterns for the meters learned on the previous page. These are four-bar phrases with fills in bar four.

 When two dynamics are listed (as in lines 4 and 5 below), it indicates to play the first dynamic the first time, then the second dynamic indication when repeating.

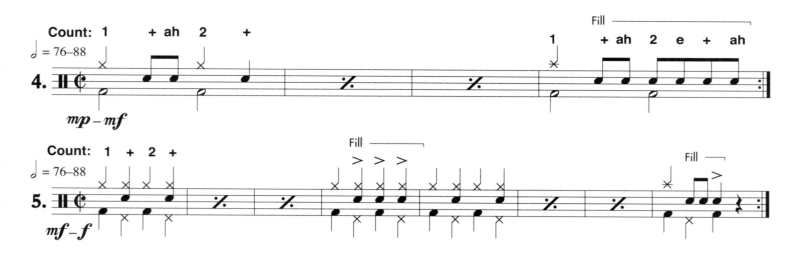

A. Practice page 50 and this page until you feel comfortable with these new meters.

B. Continue work on Technique Builder #5.

C. Continue work on rolls and triplets as necessary.

PRACTICE TIP Be sure to observe accents in lines 1–3. Also, there may be a tendency to rush these lines, particularly at slower tempos. When in doubt, check your time with a metronome or by playing along with the recording.

SPECIAL TECHNIQUES

The following techniques are part of a large body of "effects" and patterns known as **rudiments**. These include assorted rolls and certain sticking patterns. It is recommended you purchase *International Drum Rudiments* (listed on page 92) for further study.

RIM SHOTS

This is *the* loudest effect on drums (with the possible exception of a double rim shot, which is explained below). Simply strike the drum head as you normally would, but angle the stick lower so it strikes the rim simultaneously. Believe me, you'll hear it when you achieve the right sound. In music, a rim shot is often notated with an "x" (like cymbal notes) and "RS."

A double rim shot is achieved by simultaneous rim shots with both hands and is notated with two "x" noteheads.

FLAM

This is a rather subtle effect. A "principal" note is played with one hand, but a softer, "grace" note is played a fraction of a second before with the other hand.

It thickens the texture and serves as emphasis to notes—like an accent, but without the added volume.

DRAG

The drag is similar to the flam except there are two softer grace notes played before the principal note:

All of the above effects are more likely to be heard in fills and solo work, though they can be used in other instances. Care should be taken in employing these techniques—if overused, they can become ineffective and bog down the music.

FILLS USING SPECIAL TECHNIQUES

These fills will help you get the feel of how the rim shot, flam and drag may be used. It may take extra effort to master these fills. **These measures are *not* designed to be** **played one after another** as in reading a line of music. Play three measures of a basic beat you've learned in the corresponding time signature, then play the written fill in bar four. For the two-bar fills, play two bars of the basic beat, then the fill. Choose a relaxed tempo at first—one that feels comfortable. The stickings are only suggestions, and you should try your own variations. (Where sticking is not marked, try alternating hands first.)

Two-Bar Fills

Practice this page as described at the top. Work on one fill at a time until you have it memorized and can play it effortlessly. Then, go on to the next fill.

PRACTICE TIP......

Rudiments, as in the special techniques you've just learned, are regularly part of every drummer's practice sessions. Try to set aside a few minutes each time you practice to work on a few of them.

"HELP! ...

...I'm Not Coordinated"

There are three tricks used to combat the problem of playing different rhythms with hands and feet. The first you already know about: playing one rhythm, then adding another until it becomes effortless, then adding a third and so forth.

A second method is to be able to hear the parts in your head. (It has been said earlier that if you can't count it, you can't play it—similarly, if you can't *hear* it, you can't play it.) This can be related to the first trick. For instance, after having tackled only the hands, try hearing the rhythms the feet play as you play the hands.

The third trick is simple. Have a positive attitude as you practice. Regardless of how frustrating it may be to not be able to play something, just remind yourself that, with a bit more effort, there *will* be a time when the current problem—whatever it may be—will no longer exist.

...I Have No Rhythm"

In spite of what you may think, no one is born with rhythm. Though some may excel and show talent in this area, *rhythm is learned*.

Listening analytically will help you learn more quickly. When you listen to music, try to focus on the drums. What sounds do you hear? How do these sounds fit together? Try to determine precisely what the drummer is playing on the drumset. By becoming accustomed to hearing and understanding drum playing, your rhythm will naturally improve.

The previous exercises you've done in listening to drumming should not stop! **A great drummer always listens to others and learns from their playing**.

...I Have No Patience"

It may be that you do have quite a bit of coordination and rhythm—but you want to be able to play *right away*! This is natural. Everyone would love to pick up an instrument and make music effortlessly. Of course, this isn't realistic. What *is* realistic is that with time and some effort you'll be able to play drums. Patience is a virtue!

Playing Beats & Fills PART IV

This section of the book is devoted to playing assorted beats and fills, divided into five sections: Rock, Country, Jazz, Latin and "Special Requests" (beats that may be useful on gigs). While there are some simplistic patterns and fills on these pages, many will be very challenging.

PRACTICING THIS SECTION

The measures in each line on these pages are not meant to be read in succession (with the exception of the SITTING IN pages). They are to be practiced repeating any "pattern" measure three times, followed by a "fill" bar. You can mix the pattern bars with any of the "fill" bars. Where there are two-bar fills, the pattern bar should be played only twice before playing the fill. The idea is to always create four-bar phrases. You can often combine two one-bar fills to create a two-bar fill.

Again, use the methods of practice that have helped you in the past: 1) count rhythms carefully; 2) try combining two or three parts before playing an entire pattern; 3) "hear" the pattern in your head; 4) always stay relaxed. If you take a little extra time to follow these suggestions, it will payoff.

For each style, there are a few familiar songs listed to help you understand how that style sounds rhythmically. You may even want to try playing along to the original recordings of those songs—the performer is listed, rather than songwriter—which are readily available. (The album is not listed because the songs often exist on more than one album.)

While you may want to go directly to the type of music you prefer, consider going back to other styles later. You're more than likely to find that certain beats and fills may be adapted to your playing, regardless of your music style preferences.

For kits larger than four pieces: feel free to experiment using different toms when playing fills. The rhythms can be played on assorted drums and the written fills are only a sample of the style.

From the "Daily Workouts" you've seen throughout this book, you should now have a basic understanding of the nature of practice sessions. Practicing essentially consists of working on what gives you the most problems, attempting to improve your playing. The best approach is to work on one page at a time until you feel

you have it down. This may take a week or two of practicing. (The jazz and Latin sections may take more time because of the level of difficulty involved.) Then, go on to the next page.

SITTING IN and VARIATION Sections

At the end of each section there are play-along pages which coordinate with the recordings, called **"SITTING IN."** These pages put some of the assorted beats and fills into practice. You may listen to the full recording with the drums, then turn off the right channel and "sit in" as the drummer.

The **"VARIATION"** section at the bottom of some pages will give you more suggestions and ideas to further enhance your playing.

ROCK
Early
as in *Johnnie B. Goode* (Chuck Berry) and *Twist and Shout* (The Beatles).

VARIATIONS

A. Try rim shots on the snare for an extra "kick."

B. Play the hi-hat on all four beats or play the ride cymbal part on closed hi-hat.

C. Instead of constant eighth notes on the ride cymbal, occasionally mix in quarter notes.

ROCK
Hard/Metal

as in *Whole Lotta Love* (Led Zeppelin) and *Welcome to the Jungle* (Guns N' Roses)

Patterns

Fills (One-bar)

(Two-bar)

A *sforzato* is a sudden accent.

VARIATION

Experiment playing with the hi-hat on beats 2 and 4, then on all 4 beats.

ROCK
Disco/Dance

as in *Thriller* (Michael Jackson) and *Groove Is In the Heart* (Deee-Lite)

The pattern for disco or dance music primarily revolves around the following hi-hat rhythm, which emphasizes the "and" of each beat:

Patterns

A basic beat is created by adding snare and bass as follows

These next patterns incorporate sixteenths on the hi-hat. First practice snare and hi-hat before adding bass drum.

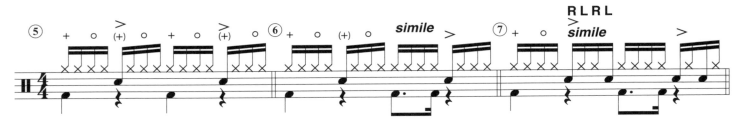

Patterns 8-10 have the right hand playing only on the "and" of each beat.

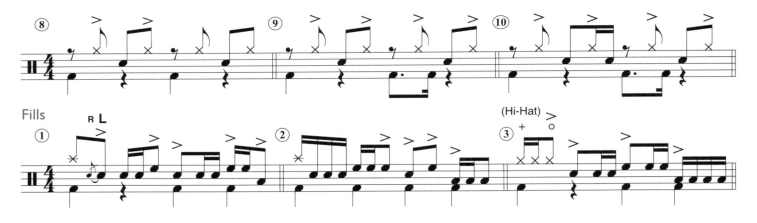

VARIATIONS

A. Play patterns 1–4 without hitting the hi-hat on the beat (only on the off beat.)

B. Practice patterns 8–11 with the hi-hat opening on the offbeat and closing on the beat as in patterns 1–4.

C Patterns 8–11 may be played with the ride-cymbal part on the bell of the cymbal or closed hi-hat. (For hi-hat, open and closed as in B.)

ROCK
Reggae (Ska)

as in *One Love* (Bob Marley & the Wailers) and recordings of Peter Tosh, and Jimmy Cliff

There is always an accent on beats two and four with the bass drum and snare, though it is not marked. As with disco/dance music, the ride cymbal part is played on the hi-hat, which is opened only when indicated.

VARIATIONS

A. Use cross-stick rim shot on the snare drum for the patterns, which is very characteristic of this musical style.

B. Try using some of the disco/dance beats, placing the bass drum on beats 2 and 4 rather than what's written.

C. As in jazz beats, swing the rhythms a bit (♫ = ♩♪)—see page 70.

ROCK

Funk   as in *Play That Funky Music* (Average White Band) and earlier Red Hot Chili Peppers music.

Of all rock styles, this is the most complex, so you'll need to take extra time with this page. The hi-hat should be used instead of the ride cymbal on patterns 1–3.

VARIATIONS

A.   Patterns 4–9 may have the ride cymbal part played on hi-hat.

B.   Try playing steady eighths, rather than quarters, on hi-hat (with foot).

ROCK
Shuffle

as in *Higher Ground* (Stevie Wonder) and, slow tempo, *Walk, Believe, Walk* (The Black Crowes)

The shuffle may be written in either $\frac{4}{4}$ or $\frac{12}{8}$ time.

Patterns

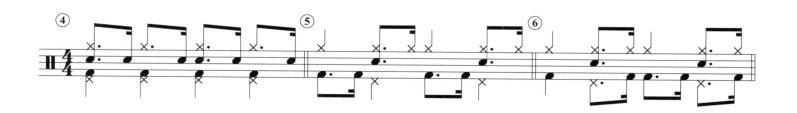

Fills

Also see JAZZ—Shuffle (page 75) for pattern and fill ideas applicable to rock-style playing.

CD Track 84

ROCK

SITTING IN

EARLY ('60s) *use any patterns and fills from page 56*

You'll note on the recording that the drummer plays quarter notes on partially open hi-hat until measure 25, then the ride cymbal is played near the bell with a mixture of quarter and eighth notes. There is no count off for "Jess's Night Out" since the guitar sets the tempo, and notice there are pick-ups at the beginning.

 MINI MUSIC LESSON When there are **multiple bars of consecutive rests**, there is a type of shorthand to indicate this (rather than having several measures of whole rests).

For example, eight bars of rests are indicated as:

8

The number above this extended rest indication tells you how many measures to rest. You'll see this at the beginning of "Jess's Night Out."

Jess's Night Out

P. Wilson

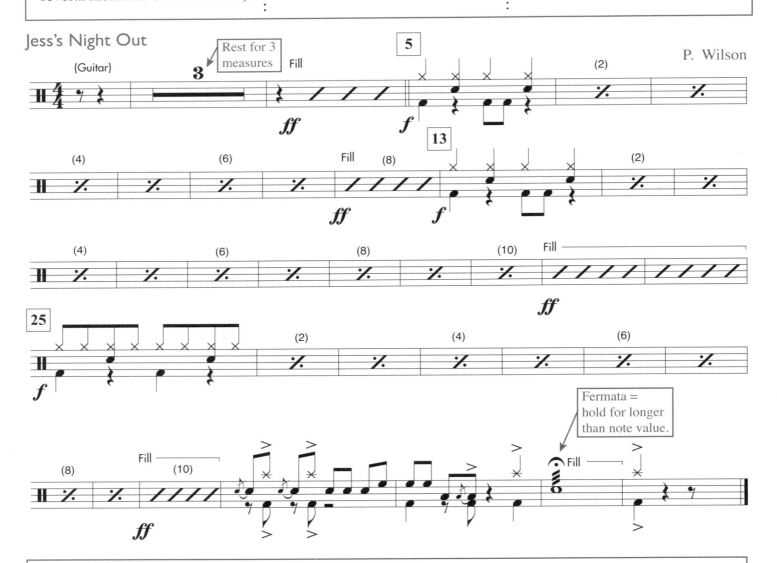

 MINI MUSIC LESSON At the end of "Jess's Night Out" is a ***fermata***; another music term derived from the Italian language. This indicates to hold a note for an unspecified length beyond the note's value. An accepted rule of thumb is to hold the note at least 1½ times its value. The fermata is encountered most often at the end of music, but also may occur at the end of a music section.

SITTING IN
ROCK

METAL *use patterns 1, 2 & 6–9 and fills 3 & 5 from page 57*

On the recording, the drummer uses a very active sixteenth-note pattern on the bass drum, which follows the bass guitar line. It is very effective, but any of the more basic patterns mentioned above will work. As "Shattered Iron" is driven by a sixteenth-note feel, sixteenth-note fills are desirable. Notice the frequent downbeat cymbal crashes on the recording, typical of this drumming style.

 The term **ad lib.** (from the Latin *ad libitum*) simply means in modern usage to be creative. When written in music, it often indicates to elaborate on a given pattern, playing what seems to fit within the context of the music. You'll see this at the end of "Shattered Iron," letting the drummer know to create a solo.

Shattered Iron

P. Wilson

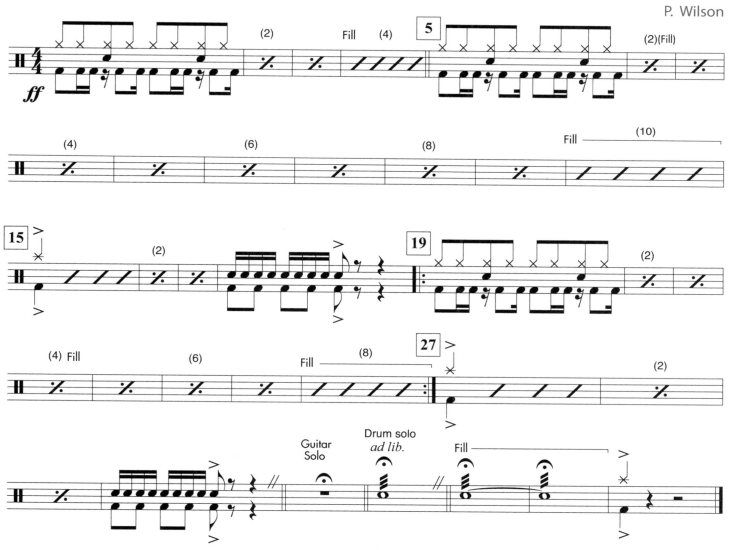

Note the slashes at the end of measures 30 and 32. These are curiously referred to as "railroad tracks." They indicate to halt the tempo, making a break or cut off before going ahead.

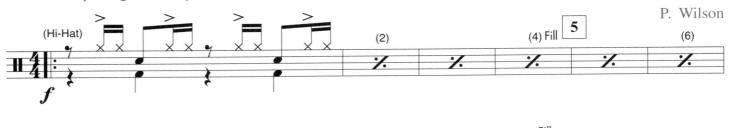

CD Track 86

ROCK

SITTING IN

REGGAE *use any patterns and fills from page 59; be sure to "swing" the rhythms (see page 70).*

On the recording, the drummer adds cowbell (mounted on the bass drum) on the repeat as interplay with the hi-hat rhythm, then uses the bell of the cymbal and, finally, returns to hi-hat. Throughout the tune, there are lively punctuations within the pattern to add rhythmic interest. **Note**: the count off on the recording equals *eighths*, not quarter notes ("1–2–3–4" = "1 & 2 &").

Better Way, Brighter Day

P. Wilson

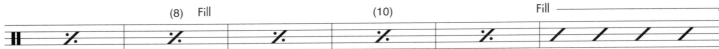

CD Track 87

FUNK *use any patterns and fills from page 60*

Basically, "Reflex" is a groove tune without a melodic line. The drummer uses a mixture of syncopated rhythms on the recording revolving around a sixteenth-note pattern.

Reflex

P. Wilson

COUNTRY

Bluegrass as in *Foggy Mountain Breakdown* (Flatt and Scruggs) and various Bill Monroe recordings

"Pure" bluegrass does not utilize drums, but nowadays drums have become somewhat accepted by the open-minded.

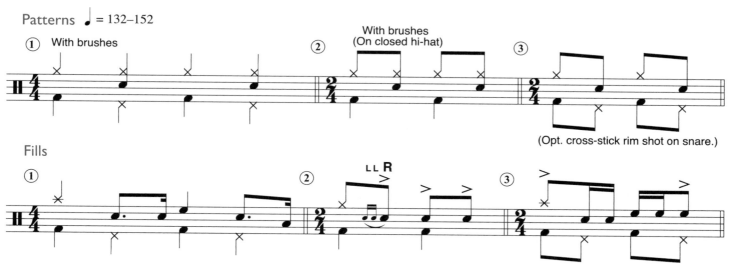

COUNTRY

Early as in *Your Cheatin' Heart* (Hank Williams) and *I'm Walkin' the Floor Over You* (Ernest Tub)

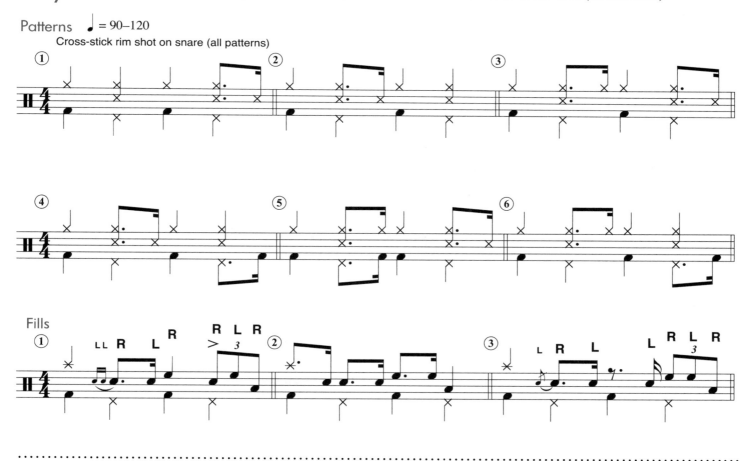

VARIATION

For the patterns, the cross-stick rim shot may be played on snare in the usual fashion.

COUNTRY
Waltz
as in *Tennessee Waltz*, *You Light Up My Life*, and *Last Chance Waltz* (various vocal artists)

COUNTRY
Shuffle (Rock-a-billy)

as in *Crazy Arms* (Jerry Lee Lewis) and *Don't Be Cruel* (Elvis Presley)

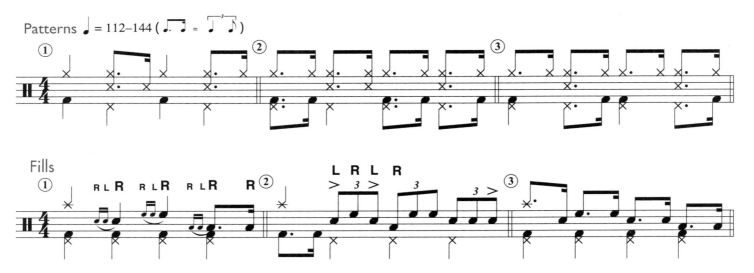

Also see ROCK—Shuffle (page 61) and JAZZ—Shuffle (page 75) for pattern and fill ideas applicable to country-style playing.

COUNTRY—Up Tempo (Fiddle Tunes)

as in *Old Joe Clark* and *Boilin' the Cabbage Down* by various fiddle artists

COUNTRY—Rock

as in *Put a Girl In It* (Brooks and Dunn) and *Girls Like Me* (Kellie Pickler)

COUNTRY—"Train" Rhythm

as in *Orange Blossom Special* (various fiddle artists) and *Folsom Prison Blues* (Johnny Cash)

VARIATION   For COUNTRY—Rock: the ride cymbal part may be played on closed hi-hat.

CD Track 88

COUNTRY

SITTING IN

WALTZ *use any patterns and fills from the top half of page 66*

Notice how the drummer on the recording reinforces the bass guitar with the bass drum in the second bar of each phrase and sometimes at the end of phrases. To keep a simple quality to the music, the fills are light in character.

In the waltz below, you'll see "***D.S. al Coda***" (D.S. is an abbreviation for the Italian *dal segno*). Read the music as you normally would until you see the "D.S." Then go back to the sign 𝄋 until you reach the second sign ⊕ At this sign, you immediately jump to the *Coda* to end the tune.

Near the end, you'll also see "***ritard.***" (another Italian abbreviation, this one for *ritardando*). It means to gradually slow the tempo. The opposite term, *accelerando*, abbreviated ***accel.***, indicates to gradually quicken the tempo.

Buckaroo Holiday Waltz

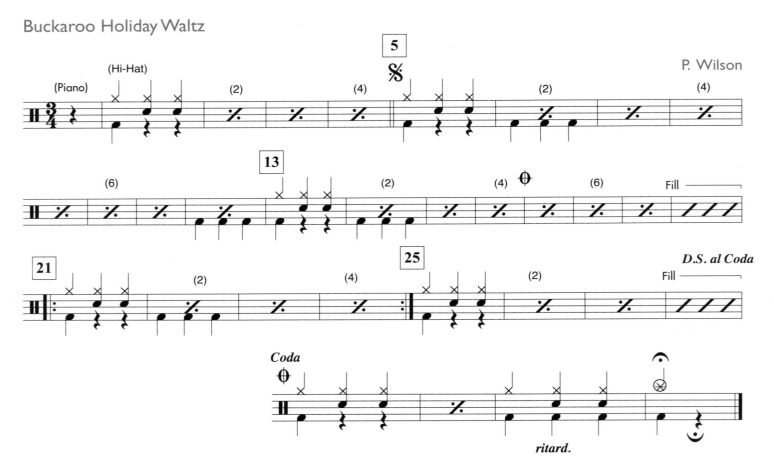

"TRAIN" RHYTHM *use any patterns and fills from the bottom of page 67*

Here, you'll encounter a ***D.C al Coda*** very similar to the *D.S. al Coda* you've just learned. The same instructions apply, except rather than repeat to a sign upon reaching "*D.C. al Coda*," you return to the beginning. (When you reach the ⊕ you go to the *Coda*, like you did with the *D.S. al Coda*.)

On the recording, the drummer occasionally chooses to change accents on the 16th-note snare rhythm. Be sure not to let the odd phrase between 29 and the ⊕ throw you off—count carefully!

SITTING IN — COUNTRY

Billy's Burlington Express

P. Wilson

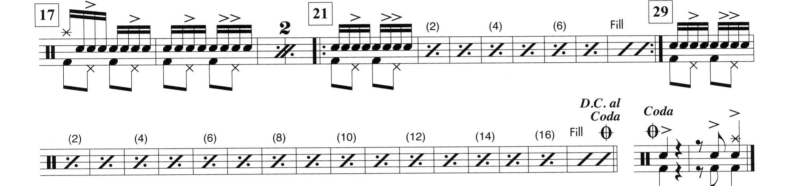

ROCK *use any patterns and fills from the middle of page 67*

Occasionally, a cymbal crash is thrown in on the recording to emphasize the end of the phrase (measures 9 and 22) or the beginning of a new one (measures 11 and 32).

Chicken Wired

P. Wilson

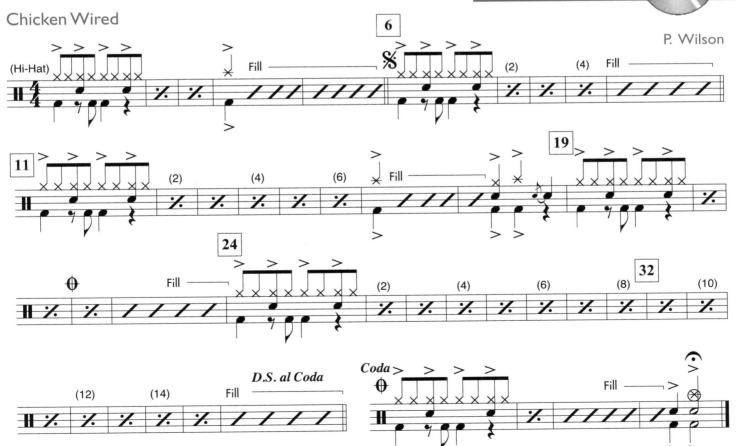

JAZZ

Jazz music, particularly of an earlier era, almost always has a "swing" feel that often employs triplet rhythms. However, the music is generally not written with triplets. As a result, the written music will often include an indication that eighth-note rhythms (or dotted eighths followed by a sixteenth) are to be played as triplets:

As a result, this written rhythm:

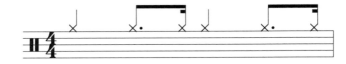

or this written rhythm:

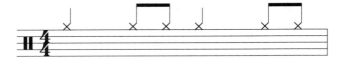

is played like:

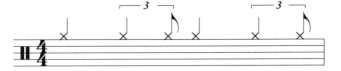

Look for the indication to "swing" the rhythms in exercises.

PLAYING "SWING" RHYTHMS ON CYMBALS

The "swing" rhythm, which is often played on the ride cymbal or hi-hat, may be executed as shown in the diagram.

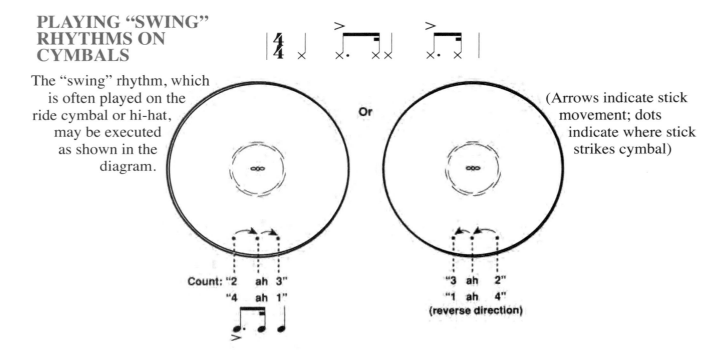

(Arrows indicate stick movement; dots indicate where stick strikes cymbal)

Because of the strong accent on beats 2 and 4 in jazz, it may feel natural to let the stick bounce to the left or right after playing on beats 2 and 4. This movement is very slight, but helps create a relaxed feel.

JAZZ—Up Tempo

as in *Seven Steps to Heaven* (Miles Davis) and *Devil May Care* (Diane Krall)

When playing faster tempos, there is a great temptation to become tense. Don't! Try to stay relaxed at all times. If you're tense, your playing will sound "tense." The dotted-eighth sixteenth rhythm (♩♪) sounds more like eighths (♫♩) the faster the tempo though, retaining a lively swing feel.

Patterns (One-bar)

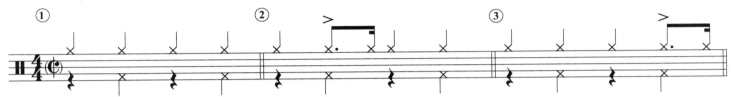

The next three patterns utilize a cross-stick rim shot. (See explanation on page 36.)

Mixing placement of the dotted-eighth, sixteenth rhythm on the cymbal is an earmark of up-tempo jazz time. But the faster the tempo, the more playing straight quarters (as in pattern 1) makes musical sense because it sounds less cluttered.

Patterns (Two-bar)

Fills

JAZZ—Blues

as in *Call It Stormy Monday* (various artists) and *I'm a Man* (Muddy Waters)

Patterns — Even though the accents are not marked, there should be an emphasis on all 4 beats, particularly on 2 and 4.

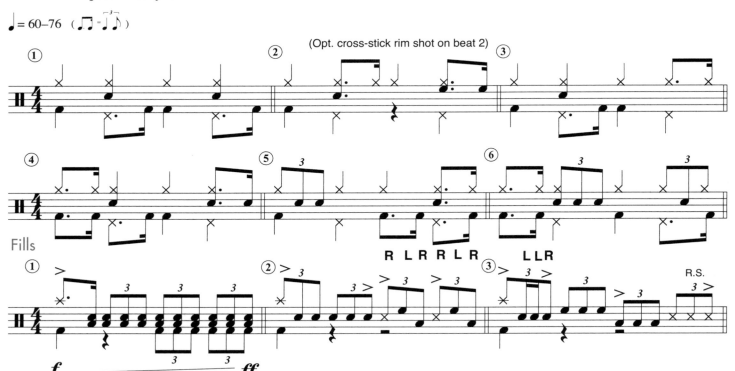

JAZZ—Dixieland

as in *When the Saints Go Marching In* and *Basin Street Blues* (as recorded by various Dixieland artists).

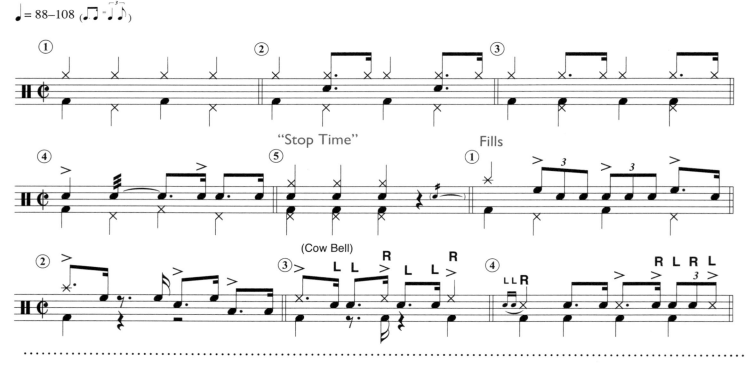

VARIATION   A. Blues: Play the ride cymbal part on hi-hat.

B. Dixieland: Ride cymbal may be played on hi-hat, opening on beats 1 and 3 for pattern.

JAZZ—Ballads

as in *When Sonny Gets Blue* and *My Funny Valentine* (various vocal and instrumental artists)

In order to create a soft, subtle rhythmic effect for jazz ballads, brushes are often used. Playing with brushes is an art because the technique is quite different from using sticks.

One of the most widely used techniques is having the left hand on the snare make a circular motion to create a continuous "swish" sound. (Note: You must have a coated snare head—not smooth plastic—to get the proper sound.) The right hand plays rhythms on the cymbals or drums.

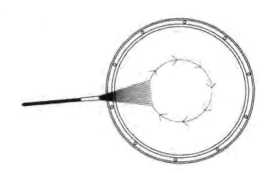

In the brush beats below, the left-hand swish sound is notated as a roll. The ride cymbal part may be played on the snare or hi-hat.

Patterns

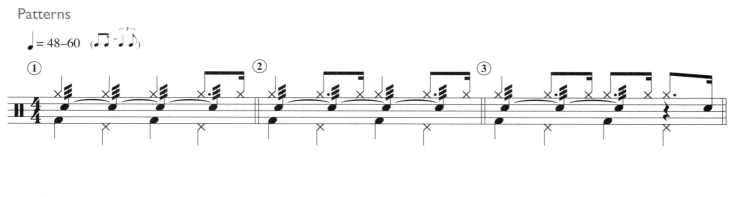

Fills

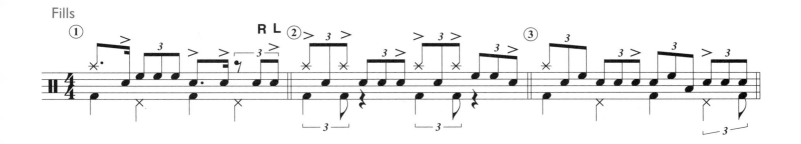

VARIATION   To keep a light sound, omit the bass drum in patterns 1–6.

JAZZ—Straight Time/Swing

as in *Satin Doll* (Duke Ellington) and *I've Got the World On a String* (various artists)

Patterns   Patterns 1–4 are typical of basic time. Patterns 5–12 may also serve as "light" fills, as well as occasional variations in time. *There should always be a slight accent on beats 2 and 4, though not always marked.* (Marked accents on beats 2 and 4 are heavier.)

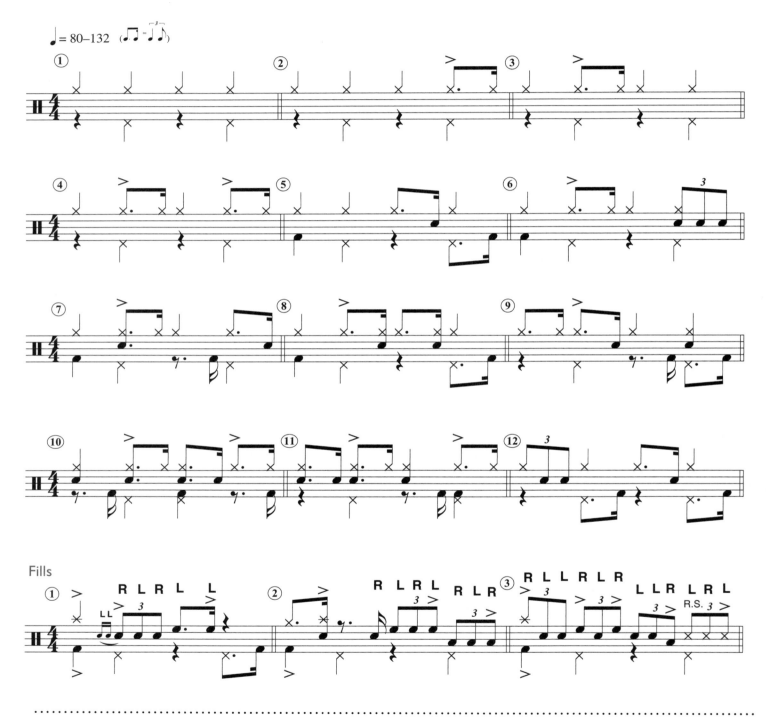

VARIATION

A. Continue mixing patterns 1–4 playing the ride cymbal rhythm (𝄽) on different beats to create new patterns.

B. Although it creates a "heavier" sound, try playing patterns 1–4 with the bass drum playing on beats 1 and 3.

JAZZ—Shuffle

as in *Night Train* (Duke Ellington) or *Just a Gigolo* (various artists).

In playing these beats be sure to accent 2 and 4 (sometimes referred to as the "back beat"). If you have difficulty, first try playing with ♩'s on the ride cymbal, rather than the ♫ rhythm.

Patterns

The shuffle may be in $\frac{12}{8}$ as well as $\frac{4}{4}$.

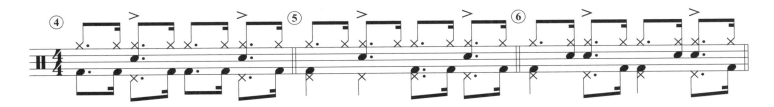

> **MINI MUSIC LESSON** The Italian term *subito*, abbreviated as **sub.**, means "suddenly" or "quickly." In music, it is commonly used before a dynamic to indicate an abrupt change of loud to soft or soft to loud.

Fills

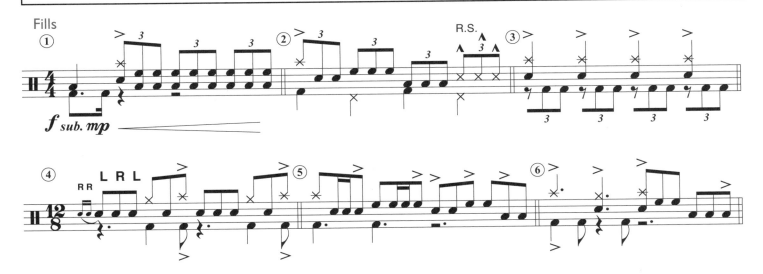

JAZZ—Waltz

as in *My Favorite Things* and *Someday My Prince Will Come* (various artists)

For this style, the tempo should be felt "in one" since it is fairly quick and should not feel heavy .

Patterns

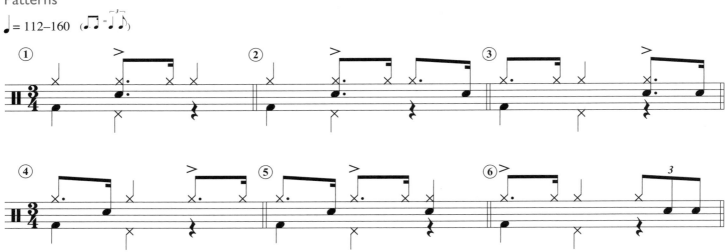

Patterns 7–9 are advanced as the hi-hat does not play on the beat.

Fills

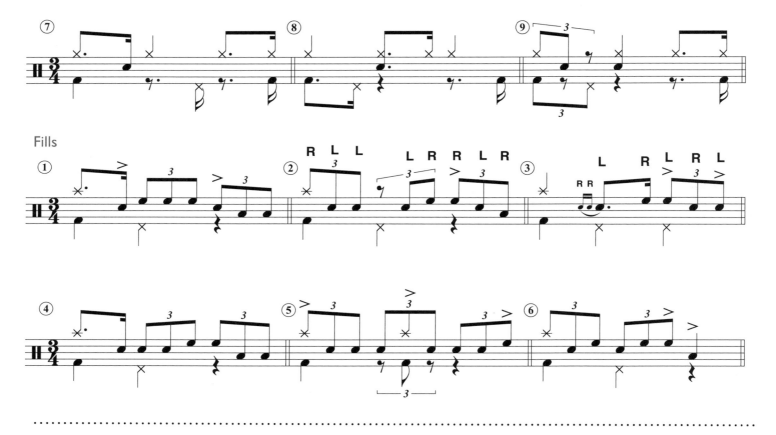

....

VARIATIONS

A. Play all patterns with brushes.

B. Play hi-hat on 3 instead of 2 on patterns 1–6.

CD Track 91

SITTING IN

JAZZ

DIXIELAND *use any patterns and fills from the bottom half of page 72*

In spots other than indicated here, the drummer includes a few light fills and accents on the recording. Also, when the melody returns after solos (at the D.S.), the backbeat is emphasized and there are more fills at the end of phrases.

When the Saints Go Marching In

J. H. Black

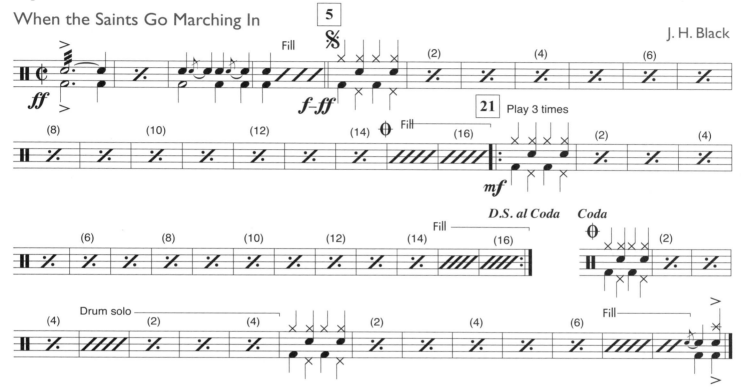

BALLAD *use any patterns and fills from page 73*

You'll notice on the recording, there is almost no bass drum, yet there is a fair amount of rhythmic activity. The key is keeping a smooth flow. This sort of playing would be totally ineffective with sticks.

CD Track 92

Left

P. Wilson

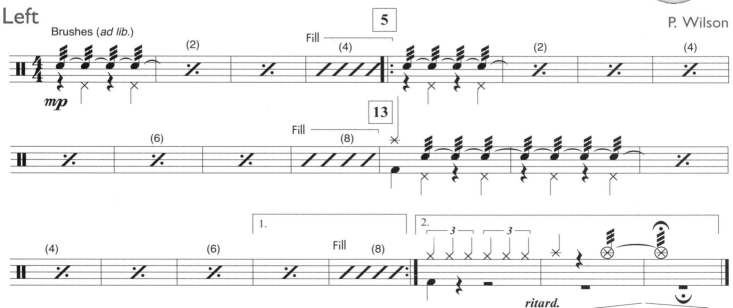

CD Track 93

JAZZ

SITTING IN

SWING & SHUFFLE *use any patterns and fills from pages 74 and 75.*

As much as this is a study in two jazz styles, this is an introduction to big-band drumming—a subject in itself! Occasionally, you'll find smaller notes above the staff which serve as cues. These indicate when the ensemble is playing; this is crucial information because the drummer needs to fill before these spots to "set up" the ensemble "kicks." Listen to how this is done on the recording. Sometimes the kicks are not set up with fills—just accented; other times there are strong 3- or 4-beat long fills before a powerful ensemble entrance. When repeating to measure 51 don't forget to switch to a shuffle beat.

Count "Knuckles" In

P. Wilson

CD Track 94

SITTING IN

JAZZ

WALTZ *use any patterns and fills from page 76*

The "combo" style of playing here is kept light in character. But the subtle additions to the basic waltz pattern heard on the recording are many. It is of particular interest to listen to only the drum track. While this is advanced playing, you should be able to pick up a few techniques to practice.

MINI MUSIC LESSON Another method of notation shorthand is simply writing an instruction that serves as music.

At measure 23 below, "Trpt Solo, Play 32 bars" is the equivalent of writing 32 measures of repeat sign for each bar. It also saves space and is easier to read!

Life in the Sahara

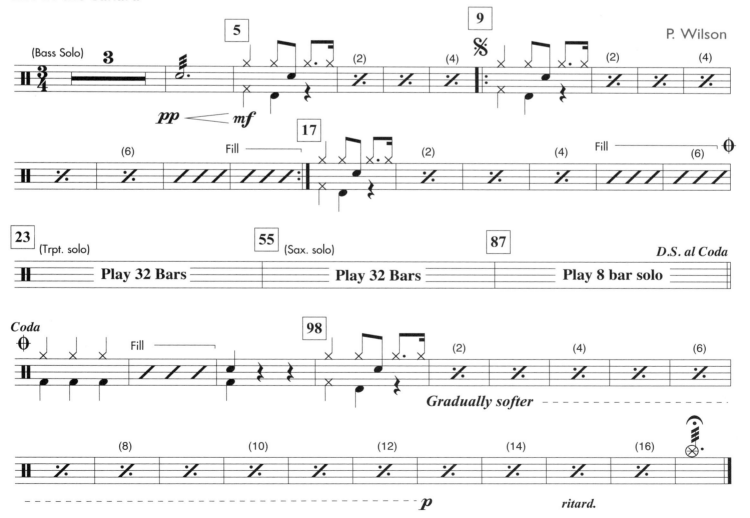

LATIN—Samba as in *One-Note Samba* (Stan Getz) or *Brazil* (various artists)

Patterns (Two-bar)

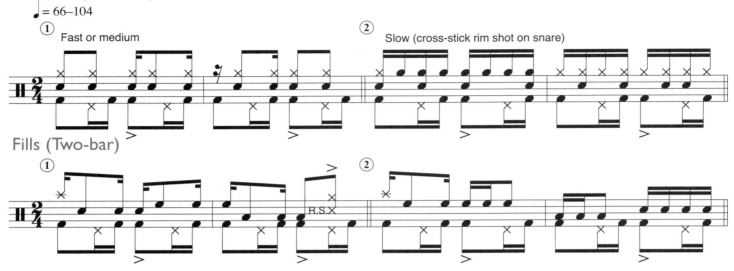

Fills (Two-bar)

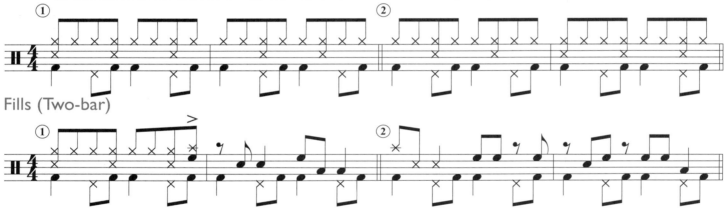

LATIN—Bossa Nova as in *Girl From Ipanema* (Joao Gilberto and others)

Patterns (Two-bar)

Fills (Two-bar)

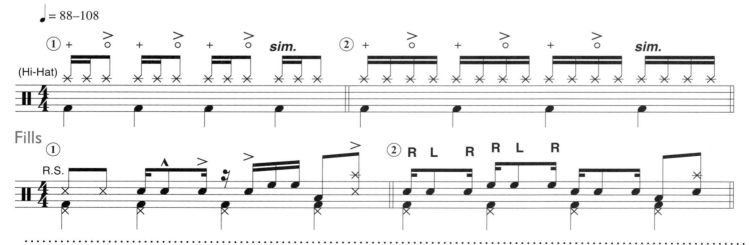

LATIN—Calypso as in music of various Trinidad steel drum bands

Patterns

Fills

VARIATIONS   Try using closed hi-hat for the ride cymbal part on Bossa Nova patterns.

LATIN—Cha Cha as often used as the style for *Tea for Two* and *Never on Sunday* (various artists)

Patterns (Two-bar)

♩ = 104–120

Fills (Two-bar)

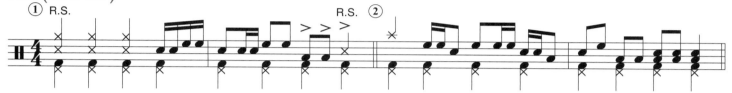

LATIN—Tango as in *Hernando's Hideaway/La Cumparsita* or *Jalonsie* (various artists)

Patterns

♩ = 96–112

Fills (Two-bar)

LATIN—Mambo

Patterns (Two-bar)

Slow ♩ = 92–132, Fast ♩ = 144–176

Fills (Two-bar)

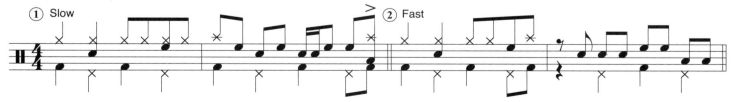

LATIN—Rumba (4/4 Bolero)

as in *The Lady in Red* and *Temptation* (various artists)

Patterns

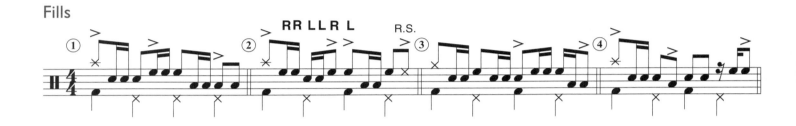

Fills

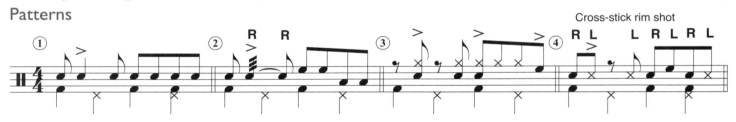

LATIN—Beguine

as in *Begin the Beguine* (various artists)

Patterns

Fills

VARIATIONS

A Play the hi-hat on all four quarter notes.

B Experiment using cross-stick rim shots, in place of snare strokes.

C Throw snares off.

CD Track 95

SITTING IN

LATIN

BOSSA NOVA *use any patterns and fills from the middle of page 80*

On the recording, there is little variation from the basic two-bar pattern. (You saw the basic pattern earlier on page 36.) Note the 16-bars are repeated twice (played a total of three times).

El Ultimo Baile ("The Last Dance")

P. Wilson

CD Track 96

CALYPSO *use any patterns and fills from the bottom of page 80*

Seed Man

P. Wilson

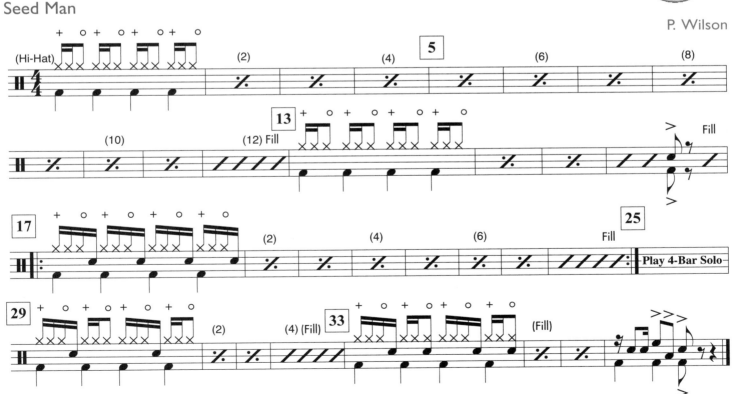

CD Track 97

LATIN   SITTING IN

CHA CHA, TANGO & RUMBA *use appropriate patterns and fills from pages 81 and 82*

This is a medley of three Latin dance beats. Each style is 16 bars long. Notice how the bass guitar lines help distinguish the three dance rhythms.

A'mour S'more

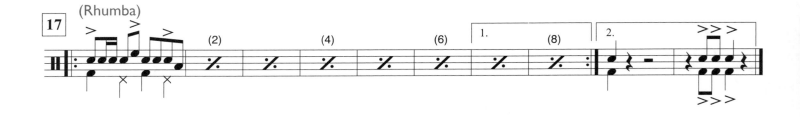

SPECIAL REQUESTS

POLKA

Pattern

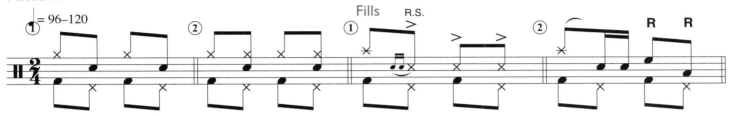

WALTZ   Also see Jazz—Waltz (page 55) and Country—Waltz (page 70).

Pattern

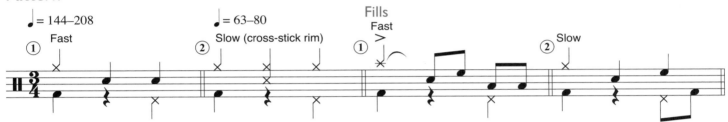

MEXICAN HAT DANCE

Pattern verse (four-bar)

Pattern chorus (two-bar)

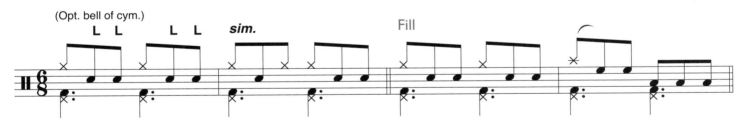

CHARLESTON   Fills from Polka, above, may be used here.

Pattern (two-, four-bar)

SPECIAL REQUESTS

CANCAN
PATTERN (TWO-BAR)

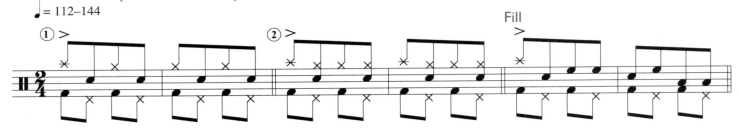

HORA There is a second section for which you may use the polka beat from the previous page.

Patterns (First-section)

IRISH JIG

Pattern (Two-bar)

TWO-STEP Polka beats may be used as well.

Patterns

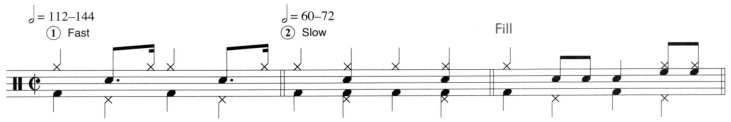

BUNNY HOP/"HOKIE-POKIE"

Pattern (Four-bar)

Odds & Ends

PART V

KEEPING YOUR EQUIPMENT IN SHAPE

Drum upkeep doesn't require much effort provided your set is in good shape to begin with. First, you should become familiar with the parts of a drum.

Probably the most regular effort will consist of changing the heads when they are worn or broken (see the next page for a guide on changing them). At this time, it is good to check for bent screws, broken snares, warped rims, faulty strainers and cracked shells. The screws should be clean and have a light coat of lubricant (such as a light grade of oil or grease, silicone spray or a dab of Vaseline).

The pedals for the bass drum and hi-hat require occasional lubrication. Once or twice a year for sets played regularly is often sufficient.

It is a good habit to cover your set when it's not in use. (This is assuming you will keep it set up in an area for daily practice and not tear it down, placing it in cases every day!) An old, but clean, sheet will protect it from dust and dirt.

The cymbals need little attention outside of an occasional polish. However, NEVER use an abrasive cleaner. There is cymbal cleaner made for polishing, but it is surprising what a little non-abrasive soap and elbow grease will do. It is important to regularly check the felts and plastic sleeves on the stands to see that they protect the cymbal from contact with the stand. *Not having the sleeves and felts can lead to a crack in your cymbal!*

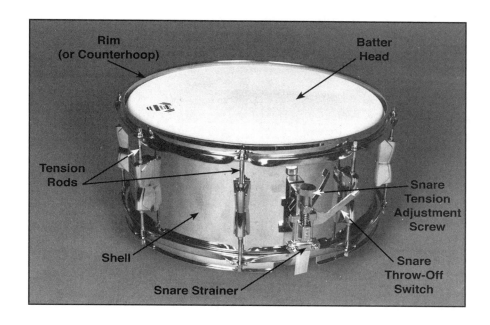

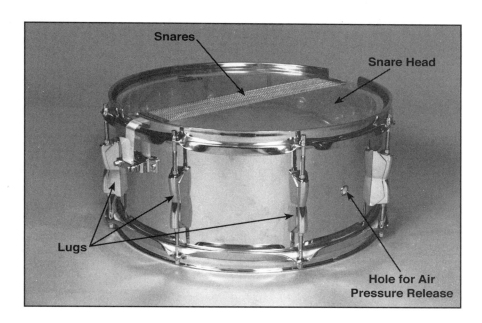

REPLACING A DRUMHEAD

The first time you break a drumhead it may seem catastrophic. You can't do much of anything on your set until the head is replaced. If you are really fearful of doing fix-it type work, one option is taking it to a music repair dealer for replacement.

If you are serious about being a drummer, however, it will be necessary—and really not so hard!—to learn how to replace a drumhead. You will need to measure the head size and specify whether it's a batter head (the side you play upon) or snare head (the *underside* of a snare drum). Heads are available in different weights and thicknesses. You may want to consult your music dealer for suggested replacement, depending on the type of drum and the sort of sound you want. Following these steps will make changing a head relatively painless:

1. With your drum key (or a drum wrench), loosen all the screws, but do not pull the screws out of the hoop.

2. Lift the hoop away from the shell leaving the screws hanging loose in the hoop holes.

3. Remove the bad head from the shell.

4. Check wood-shell rims for any imperfections. Take it to a service professional for correction rather than attempting to sand it (which will ruin the rim).

5. Wipe the shell clean with an *only slightly* damp, clean cloth. Wipe it again with a dry cloth. (It may be a good idea to turn the drum upside down and shake it a bit to get rid of any foreign objects or dust inside.)

6. Place the new head on the rim, making sure it fits firmly against the rim.

7. Place the hoop over the head, again making sure it fits snugly over the head.

8. With your fingers, screw the screws into place. (If needed, clean and lubricate the screws with grease or a dab of Vaseline before replacing). The screws should be tightened only with slight finger pressure.

9. Selecting any lug, start tightening the screws making two full turns with the drum key or wrench, working in a pattern across the drum as shown: called cross-tension tuning.

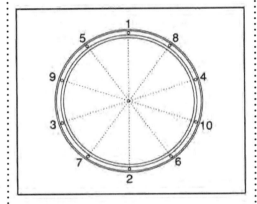

10. Repeat this pattern. If it seems two full turns may be too much, reduce it to one or one-and-a-half turns.

11. Repeat this pattern as much as is necessary to achieve the correct tension, reducing the amount of the turn at each lug with each repetition of the pattern. Between each pattern, apply pressure with your palm in the center of the head in order to let the head "seat" with the edge of the drum. Check the tension by tapping the drumhead.

Fine tuning can be done by tapping at the edge of the drum near each individual lug. Lightly place a finger in the center to eliminate unwanted overtones. Listen to the pitch. If it is higher than the others, loosen the lug slightly, apply pressure to the head momentarily with your palm and tap again. If it is lower in pitch, tighten the lug slightly. Continue tapping and adjusting until the pitch is the same at each lug. When this process is completed, you're ready to get back to playing! (Note: It is normal for the drumhead to stretch a bit over time, so you may want to check your drum and fine tune once a day until the stretching stabilizes over a few days.)

One final note: There is often the fear that when you tighten a head, it's going to pop like a balloon because of crackle sounds. This almost never happens. Heads are tested to withstand an enormous amount of pull. In the rare occurrence that you tighten a head and it breaks, the head may have been defective to begin with. Consider taking it back to the dealer and asking for a replacement.

TUNING

There are almost as many approaches to tuning drums as there are players. It is a very important consideration since it has much to do with creating "your sound." Because it is a personal preference, no one can tell you how your drums should be tuned. The type of heads you use (discussed below), muffling (see page 16), the type of music you play and your own taste will be factors. However, there are some tips that may help you achieve the sound you are looking for. As with other aspects of drumming, much will be accomplished through experimentation.

First, it is desirable to have even tension at each lug. Any turning of a screw should be duplicated with all screws (assuming that there is even tension across the head to begin with). To check this, slightly muffle the drumhead with your finger at the center and tap close to the rim at each point where there is a screw. (The opposite head should be completely muffled and if you're checking the snare, the snares should be off.) If the pitch is the same, there is even tension. At those points where the pitch is lower or higher, tighten or loosen the screw to match pitches. Do this with both heads on each drum.

You will want to consider the relationship of pitches between each drum. Ordinarily, the snare is the highest pitched drum and the bass drum is the lowest. One approach would be to first find the sounds you like with these two drums, then tune the toms between the snare and bass. (If you have a large set with many toms, you may want the smallest tom equal to or even higher than the snare, but this would be a rather exceptional situation.) The toms are tuned highest to lowest with respect to their size.

You may not want to tune both heads on a drum to the same pitch. On the snare drum, it is usually preferable to tune the top batterhead lower than the snarehead. With toms, tuning the top head higher than the bottom will make the pitch bend upward. Tuning the top head lower than the bottom creates more projection of the drum sound. The common approach with the bass drum heads is to tune the head that is played upon higher in pitch than the front head. Again, there are no hard-and-fast rules, so experiment.

At the end of the recording, you will hear the individual sounds of each drum. This is only for reference purposes, giving you an idea of how one professional chooses to tune. If you feel your set is poorly tuned, this reference can serve as a starting point for tuning your kit. The sounds you will hear are unmuffled. Some degree of muffling, at least for the bass drum, will be desirable.

DRUMHEADS

Drumheads are available in different weights and styles. As with tuning, the type of music played and sound desired, along with the volume at which the drummer tends to play, will be deciding factors in the choice of heads.

Thin heads have more attack and tone, and project more, than thick heads. Thick heads have less projection, but a dull attack and little ring. (Of course, the amount of ring can be modified with muffling.) A thicker head will endure heavier playing more than thin heads. As you would expect, medium heads characteristically fall in the middle.

Over the years, special heads, such as "hydraulic" (containing fluid to dampen sound), sound dots (a round dampening patch in the center) and pin stripes (which is a sort of two-ply head) have been manufactured. Generally, transparent and smooth-coated white heads are favored by many because of their superior tone. Jazz drummers often use a rough-coated batterhead on the snare for effective use of brushes.

BEING YOUR OWN TEACHER

In order to teach yourself to play drums, you must play the dual role of student and teacher. Here are a few suggestions for approaching this role.

READ THE BOOK

Yes, if you wanted to read, you would have gone to the library. Because you want to *play* the drums, you may be tempted to use only the CD and just play along with the SITTING IN sections. There is nothing terribly wrong with that. You *will* learn much by playing along and…*it's fun*! (*That* may be your sole purpose for learning to play.) However, you will get only so far using just one portion of this method.

The more you want to improve your playing, the greater the importance of taking advantage of what the text has to offer. Don't hesitate to reread those sections you find valuable. But be sure to read everything at least once.

USE YOUR PRACTICE TIME SENSIBLY

Most of life's learning activities stress fundamentals. The problem is they are not much fun. This doesn't necessarily have to be the case.

The drudgery of working on the basics—and it *is* work!—can be successfully intermingled with more enjoyable aspects of playing … like playing along with recordings or just banging out some beats you know and love to play. Many students find success by dividing their practice time between work and reward. You should begin practicing by warming up with one or two Technique Builders. Then, the focus of your practice session should be whatever has given you the most difficulty in prior practice sessions. Then, after having spent the majority of your practice time working through problem areas, reward yourself by playing for pure fun. This means coping with the evil "D" word, discipline, but it pays off!

PAY ATTENTION TO WHAT YOU'RE DOING

Stop and think for a moment about what a teacher does. Essentially, a teacher observes, analyzes and passes constructive criticism on to the student. While you will not have the knowledge and experience of a competent drum teacher, you can observe, analyze and correct certain problems if you keep your eyes and ears open.

TAKE TIME

You may have a tendency to rush through one page after another in a race to get through the book. This will get you nowhere fast. You will be cheating yourself out of the opportunity to learn. If you are serious about playing, you will allow time to learn one page before moving on to the next one. Obviously, some people will get through the course faster than others. There is enough information and exercises in these pages to provide even the most talented beginner with many months of study.

THINK REALISTICALLY

Everyone hopes to be a success at whatever endeavor they undertake. Your dream may be to buy a drumset, sit down and, in a week or two, be playing in front of thousands of screaming fans. Maybe you will eventually become a fine drummer. But don't expect this to happen overnight. Not one drummer has achieved any success without paying his or her dues. If you want to make this a fun hobby, put in whatever time pleases you. If your goal is to make this a career—even as an amateur—you'll need to get serious about maintaining your practice schedule.

WHERE TO GO FROM HERE

FINDING A TEACHER

If you are hooked on learning to play and are considering taking lessons, here are some things to ask yourself and others when selecting a teacher:

1. Does the teacher have experience in teaching and playing?

2. How many students study with the teacher? Can you speak with any of the students currently studying with the teacher? How do they feel about the instruction they've received?

3. Are there professional musicians or teachers who recommend the teacher?

4. What are the fees for the instruction? Are there any discount "packages" that the teacher offers?

Living in a large city will give you more options in your search. Take your time. If you don't feel comfortable with the teacher after a few lessons, for whatever reason, you may want to try another instructor.

ATTEND CLINICS

In larger cities at music stores and at universities, workshops and clinics may occasionally be held. Big-name artists sometimes appear at these seminars, sharing their valuable knowledge. Check with the music stores and the music department at universities in your area to see if they have plans to hold a drumset clinic.

READ DRUM AND MUSIC MAGAZINES

There are several magazines available, either through subscription or purchase from your local music dealer, to help you further you skills. Magazines (such as *Modern Drummer*) include interviews with artists, playing tips, new equipment info, question and answer columns, etc. But don't overlook other music magazines, which often include valuable information for drummers as well.

JOIN P.A.S.

The Percussive Arts Society is an international organization committed to the education of percussionists and drummers, from beginner to professional. Membership includes a subscription to *Percussive Notes* magazine, admittance to the P.A.S.I.C. (the annual international convention that is held in a different major city each year) and more. If you ever have the opportunity to attend the P.A.S.I.C., the exposure to several days of clinics with the world's top drummers and percussionists, unusual concerts and the latest equipment is simply joyously overwhelming. For more information, write to P.A.S., 110 W. Washington Street, Suite A, Indianapolis, IN 46204 (www.pas.org).

CHECK OUT OTHER INSTRUCTION BOOKS

There are many instruction books available to help you continue your studies. Your local music dealer can assist you in finding a book that is right for you. On the next page is a listing of some of the books you may want to review.

OTHER USEFUL ALFRED DRUMSET & PERCUSSION PUBLICATIONS

30-Day Drum Workout (Book and DVD) (24210) *Pete Sweeney*
Packed with two complete 30-day exercise routines, this collection of warm-ups, sticking exercises, polyrhythms and other skill-builders increases coordination, stamina, finesse and sense of time without the tedium of doing the same old routine every day.

Advanced Funk Studies (Book and 2 CDs) (94-RLP1) *Rick Latham*
Included in Modern Drummer magazine's list of the 25 greatest drum books, Advanced Funk Studies will help take your groove to the next level. With author and renowned drummer Rick Latham as your guide, you'll learn hi-hat, funk, and fill patterns.

The Commandments of R & B Drumming (Book and CD) (0110B) *Zoro*
The Commandments of R&B Drumming is a historical and in-depth study of R&B drumming, from soul to funk to hip-hop, written by world-renowned session & live drummer Zoro (Lenny Kravitz, Bobby Brown, Sean Lennon). Topics include practice tips, developing the funky bass drum and hi-hat, creating and playing with loops, and what are considered the Ten Commandments of Soul, Funk, and Hip-Hop.

The Commandments of Early Rhythm and Blues Drumming (Book and CD) (30555) *Zoro & Daniel Glass*
Eight years in the making, this "prequel" to The Commandments of R&B Drumming delves into the rhythm and blues of the 1940s and 1950s, an incredible musical era when shuffles ruled the airwaves and modern groove playing was in its infancy. Written by Zoro and Daniel Glass (Royal Crown Revue), this book includes the most comprehensive guide to shuffle playing ever written.

The Coordination Code (38885) (Book and MP3 CD) *Karl Sloman*
The Coordination Code uses a unique system of notation to teach your body to achieve complete coordination when performing two or more movements at one time, and gain a new set of tools to utilize in your playing.

Drum Backbeats Encyclopedia (Book and CD) (20401) *John Thomakos*
This book provides hundreds of useful backbeats for the drumset. You will learn to play backbeat grooves with solid time and good feel. Beats are shown with essential variations and embellishment. Rock, blues, pop, funk, soul and many other styles are included. There are lessons on muscle memory, practice, ghost notes, open hi-hat, hi-hat with foot.

Drummer's Guide to Fills (Book and CD) (30251) *Pete Sweeney*
Drummer's Guide to Fills is designed to expand drumming vocabulary by teaching fills all drummers can use to add excitement to different sections of a song, or even use as the building blocks of a solo. Learn fills in many styles, from rock to funk to jazz, plus a "melodic" approach to fills that allows further embellishment on basics.

The Drummer's Toolkit (Book and DVD) (22646) *Dave Black*
In addition to the nuts-and-bolts details of topics such as each drum and its parts, tuning techniques, and the steps for changing a drumhead, you'll learn how to choose between the various types of heads, cymbals, and drumsticks to get just the sound you want, arrange your drumset in a way that's right for you, and make adjustments and repairs that will keep your equipment in prime condition.

Drumset Method Complete (36171) (Book and MP3 CD) *Pete Sweeney*
Anyone interested in playing the drumset can pick up this well-paced, comprehensive method and get started right away. Beginning to advanced concepts include stick techniques, rudiments, accents, swing eighths, shuffle beats, the flam and drag, building endurance, multiple-bounce rolls, sixteenth-note funk beats, and examples in many styles.

Essential Drum Lessons with the Greats (35141) (Book and CD) *John Xepoleas*
This outstanding book includes in-depth lessons, and two lesson-matching CDs are included so every percussionist can study and hear the grooves, fills, techniques, and concepts of Tim Alexander, Kenny Aronoff, Gregg Bissonette, Peter Erskine, Neil Peart, Mike Portnoy, Steve Smith, and Dave Weckl. The CDs feature performances by the drummers themselves.

Essential Styles for the Drummer and Bassist, Book 1 (Book and CD) (4309) *Steve Houghton & Tom Warrington*
A unique book/CD package which gives you the opportunity to play along with some of today's top studio musicians, while you learn to play a variety of popular grooves including pop-rock, funk, R & B, fusion, Latin and jazz. Musical charts of each selection on the CD along with essential patterns and performance/listening suggestions are included.

International Drum Rudiments (Book and CD) (18048) *Rob Carson & Jay Wanamaker*
This is the new official rudiment list as adopted by the Percussive Arts Society. A recording performed by World Champion Snare Drummer, Rob Carson, is included.

On the Beaten Path (Book and CD) (28006) *Rich Lackowski*
This must-have guide for drummers provides insight into the history and development of a wide selection of genres, including funk, alternative/punk rock, metal, progressive rock, classic rock, jam band, fusion, jazz, and reggae, and explores the legendary drummers that affected each style. Includes beats and solos from songs by Led Zeppelin, The Who, Rush, Metallica, The Police, Dream Theater, and others.

The Pro Drummer's Handbook (Book and CD) (19432) *Pete Sweeney*
Covering everything from technique and effective practice to passing an audition and how to make it as a freelance drummer, this comprehensive guide is the ultimate reference for any aspiring professional drummer looking for advice on playing the drums and surviving in the music business.

Progressive Steps to Syncopation for the Modern Drummer (Book) (17308) *Ted Reed*
Voted second on Modern Drummer's list of 25 Greatest Drum Books in 1993, *Progressive Steps to Syncopation for the Modern Drummer* is one of the most versatile and practical works ever written for drums. Created exclusively to address syncopation, it has earned its place as a standard tool for teaching beginning drummers syncopation and strengthening reading skills.